LANDSCAPES
FOR
LEARNING

Creating Outdoor Environments
for Children and Youth

Sharon Stine

California State Polytechnic University, Pomona, California

JOHN WILEY & SONS, INC.

New York   Chichester   Brisbane   Toronto   Singapore   Weinheim

Library of Congress Cataloging-in-Publication Data

Stine, Sharon.
    Landscapes for learning : creating outdoor environments for
children and youth / by Sharon Stine.
            p.   cm.
    Includes bibliographical references and index.
    ISBN 0-471-16222-1 (cloth : alk. paper)
    1. School grounds—Design—Case studies.   2. School grounds—
Psychological aspects—Case studies.   3. School environment—Case
studies.   4. Outdoor education—Case studies.   I. Title.
LB3251.S696   1996
    371.6′ 1—dc20   96-20212

Printed in the United States of America

10   9   8   7   6   5   4   3   2   1

To our grandchildren
who need protected habitats for play
in this next millennium

To the dedicated designers and teachers
who together will create meaningful outside places
for our children and youth

CONTENTS

OVERVIEW

When visiting the site of the 1992 Expo in Seville, Spain, I was struck by the contrast between outside and inside space—its design and purpose. Outside, in the frying-pan heat of the summer Andalusian sun, I was canopied by lush, lacy green plants supported by steel frames. Jets of misty water created overhead rhythms of cooling air. Down the center ran a pathway, a fragrant, protected outside space. The overhead structures, although elaborate in design and technology, provided simply places for pausing to regain body comfort. They formed circulation links to the important places—the buildings. There, in carefully controlled air-conditioned interiors was Spain's exposition, where I would learn about a country's rich cultural heritage. Yet it was outside in these walk-through areas where I could watch people and delight in the passing parade of the world's cultures. It was here that my senses were bombarded by the bright intensity of Seville's sun and sky, the smells of olive oil, the rhythm of other languages. Exposure was direct and its sensory input rich. Here, outside, I learned spontaneously about Spain, its people, culture, and history.

So often we discount the potential of outside space as a setting for learning. The outside areas of schools are frequently neglected or seen as places to pause between lessons learned inside. This book is about the creation of outdoor settings that are part of the entire educational experience.

I have focused on school environments where space is more than just useful or safe, but part of the fabric of learning and a rich reflection of layers of culture.

> ◆ *We also think that the space has to be a sort of aquarium that mirrors the ideas, values, attitudes, and cultures of the people who live within it.*
>
> —Malaguzzi 1984

A purpose of this book is to help designers and teachers think about the quality of outside school environments as learning places. It is outdoors that the ebb and flow of spontaneous activities can take place. Re-thinking the outside space means considering its potential for rich sensory input, flexible furnishing, and endless possibilities for exploration. It means creating a valued place where children and adults learn because it "mirrors the ideas, values, attitudes, and cultures of those who live there."

This book is also the result of curiosity—my curiosity about adults who work with and create environments for children. What supports or inhibits designers and teachers in the creation of educational settings? How do different adults describe and relate to the same outside space that includes trees, asphalt, grass, cement, fencing, and sand? What makes a school environment endure over time with a special sense of place? What common language can both teacher and designer use in the creation of outside school environments for children?

This book has a long and personal history. As researcher, faculty member, and administrator (Stine 1983) I have spent time over many years "hanging out" with kids; watching, taking notes, questioning, and writing about how adults create settings for children. It has been helpful to approach this work from a dual perspective: first, from my training in human development and early childhood education; and second, from a later-added design background. The case studies, results of interviews, and discoveries presented here are written for both the teacher and the designer. My observing and learning from both groups of professionals as they think through the quality of outside space is the core of this book.

We begin with the players: The designer, a "maker" of school form, the teacher, the "maintainer" of the environment, and the child, who is often a major force in "messing-up" the space. All interact, and their interaction impacts the planning, building, and use of outside educational environments. These three players, their roles, and interactions are described in Chapter 1. The forces that shape the players' interaction is examined and the characters are cast in new ways that challenge the limits of gender or professional role stereotypes.

When making any journey, I try to familiarize myself with some of the basic polite or needed survival words of the unfamiliar culture. It helps me make connections, open dialog, and react with greater sensitivity to those who live there. Even when we speak the same language, we are limited by the ways words define our particular work. Words may help make connections but can also cause separations. All professions have "their own" words. These words separate the doctor from the patient, the lawyer from the client, the teacher from the designer. A common vocabulary is needed to support collaborative work. Chapter 2 places the players in a setting and, by describing the dimensions of this setting, explores a common vocabulary. The nine pairs of contrasting elements essential in any play environment are introduced in this chapter and form the foundation of a shared language. This basic vocabulary or common analytical language can be used by the players to analyze outside space and to better understand what is missing for both children and adults who experience the environment.

How do we get from here to there—what is the process? Teachers are pressured to focus on results, products, what has been learned, completed. Designers are asked to create things, generate built forms, products. Both groups of professionals value the processes of design and teaching; however, results are often the focus. And yet the journey, the process, teaches. For the child, it is the journey that is filled with magic, wonder, and endless possibilities. Unfortunately for the adult, journeys may be like airplane flights, filled with uncomfortable problems and constrained by time segments to be simply endured rather than savored.

Consider my trip from Chihuahua, Mexico, to Albuquerque, New Mexico. The lack of direct flights provided an opportunity to explore. With abundant time between my arrival in Chihuahua and airplane departure from El Paso airport later the same day, I took a bus to the Mexican–USA border. My journey was transformed. No longer was I seat-belt secure with predictable beverage service and repeated FAA formula announcements. The bus trip was rich with the comings and goings of people, their wares, sounds, sights, and smells. The icy lime of a frozen juice bar was a welcome taste of tart coolness. Songs accompanied by guitar chords and colorful souvenirs surrounded me. These things enriched my journey and kept me in touch with people and their culture while en route to the border between Mexico and the United States. Understanding a journey, what happens en route, studying the process by which something develops and changes over time, is as important as evaluating the product itself.

Chapter 3 describes a journey, the process. Long-term case studies tell the story of the development of outside space in two schools over an 80-year time span. Both of these environments, a high school and a preschool/elementary school, have endured over time with a special "sense of place" (Proshansky , Fabian, and Kamenoff 1983). Chapter 3 does not present a study of attachment to place. This has been carefully researched and presented by others (Cooper Marcus 1992; Chawla 1994; Downing 1992; Hart 1979; Moore 1990; Proshansky, Fabian, and Kamenoff 1983, 1987). It is the intent of this chapter that designers and educators will profit from an understanding of the history or process of developing an educational environment over time. Readers are invited to learn from our past, from the wisdom of those who created, changed and nourished an educational setting. How, when, and why have these 80-year-old school environments changed? Through the history of these "particular places" that are still cherished by those who work there, the teachers' role and the design process over time are described and compared.

I know when something fits, when the clothing I wear meets my physical and social comfort needs. Discovering a good fit is a process of problem solving: selection, trying on, and evaluating. Choosing something to wear may be limited by the expertise of a fashion designer or tailor, resources, need, comfort, and personal preference, but I try to control the "fit". The process of finding a "fit" between a physical setting and those who use it includes similar challenges and problems. Control may shift between designer, teacher, and child. Resources, needs, and comfort vary vastly between young people and adults, and personal preferences, values, and goals impact the choice making of all three players. Chapter 4 presents an analysis of this process of finding a fit or congruence (Barker 1968; Prescott 1975) between a physical setting and the users of that setting. The analysis is aided by four contrasting case studies: an art studio, a preschool located on church property, an Armenian school, and a children's museum. The analysis of the design and development process described in previous chapters is further explored within the descriptions that describe each of these outside settings.

Four elements are suggested as guides, as signs en route, for designers and educators who embark on their journey to find a fit between a physical environment and its users.

It is in experiencing an unfamiliar place like Spain or Mexico that I learn more about my own values, behaviors, and culture. The continual contrasts of food, social interaction, and built forms which ask me to behave with sensitivity to what may seem foreign or strange, put the familiar in question. Analysis of these questions raised helps me arrive at greater clarity in my thinking. It forces me to ask, Why? When invited to spend time teaching at a small college on the island of Kyushu in Japan, I found my beliefs about children's environments constantly challenged by the new questions my Japanese students asked and by those I asked myself. Observing children and teachers use their environment caused a reexamination of my assumptions about the ways physical design supports children's learning through play. Subsequent visits, observations, and interviews have stimulated my thinking as I continue to explore our differences. Chapter 5 opens with a case study of a Japanese kindergarten environment. Four design elements, drawn from my research and illustrated by the case study, are summarized and their implications analyzed. This chapter challenges teachers and designers to look through a contrasting cultural lens to consider fresh ways of thinking about the creation of settings for young people in the United States.

The first five chapters of this book focus on the design of outside spaces for young people. Chapter 6, however, takes a different pathway and focuses on adults who spend a major portion of their working day in educational settings.

In any return to a particular place, we experience it as familiar but notice differences, details that were, perhaps, missed when first passing through. On a first visit to Spain, the smell of olive oil may dominate my sensory experience of Spanish food, but during a second trip I become more aware of the endless varieties of the olive itself: dark, rich, almost sea-like in Berja; bitter, hard, soil-like in Nijar. Likewise, different awareness of design dimensions is possible in viewing a setting for children through the study of adults' needs and preferences. What do adults need outside and why? What are adults naturally attracted to outside and what do they avoid? What do adults like to do outside? What is *basic* for the adult who works with children? Chapter 6 draws on research in a variety of educational settings that studied adult responses to questions of this type. Analyzing outside space in this way allows a design process in which adult activities are included in what is basic. Using adult needs as criteria, the nine pairs of elements presented in

Chapter 2 are analyzed and reconfigured. This new focus highlights five of the pairs as particularly important from an adult point of view.

The final chapter reflects on the potential of outside spaces to be safe settings for learning. The social problems of today frequently mean that backyards, blocks, lots, woods, pathways are no longer habitats that children can safely explore. It is increasingly difficult for youth to find opportunities for contact with the natural world. School grounds are potentially secure outdoor places that could be redesigned to provide such experiences. Four case studies illustrate ways to transform school grounds into safe, interesting places that connect our young people to this earth. Involving children and youth as equal partners in making changes to outdoor environments is illustrated in case study examples that describe preschool, elementary, and high school settings.

In creating outdoor environments there are problems that have no easily defined answers, no "six easy steps"; therefore, this book describes journeys, relationships, roles, and change processes. My goal is to provide descriptive tools for both teachers and designers that will support them as they solve problems so that ultimately our children and youth, who spend a majority of their years in educational settings, can be the beneficiaries of this collaboration. This book offers a challenge to designers, teachers, and young people to work together in this next millennium, to revisit outside educational environments, and to transform them into meaningful places that grow over time.

References

Barker, Roger. 1968. *Ecological Psychology*. Palo Alto, CA: Stanford University Press.

Chawla, Louise. 1994. *In the First Country of Places: Nature, Poetry and Childhood Memory*. Albany, NY: State University of New York Press.

Cooper Marcus, Clare. 1992. "Environmental memories." *In Place Attachment*, edited by I. Altman and S. Low. New York: Plenum Press.

Downing, Frances. 1992. "The role of place and event imagery in the act of design." *The Journal of Architectural and Planning Research* 9:1, 64–77.

Hart, Roger. 1979. *Children's Experience of Place*. New York: Irvington Press.

Malaguzzi, Loris. 1984. *L'occhio se salta il muro*. Catalog of the exhibit, "L'occhio se salta il muro," published by the Comune di Reggio Emilia, Assesserato Istruzione, Regione di Emilia Romagna.

Moore, Robin. 1990. *Childhood's Domain*. Berkeley, CA: MIG Communications.

Proshansky, Harold, Abbe Fabian, and R. Kamenoff. 1983. "Place and identity." *Journal of Environmental Psychology* 3: 57–83.

Prescott, Elizabeth. 1975. *Assessment of Child Rearing Environments: An Ecological Approach.* Pasadena, CA: Pacific Oaks College.

Proshansky, H. and A. Fabian. 1987. "The development of place identity in the child." In *Spaces for Children: The Built Environment and Child Development*, edited by C. Weinstein and T. David. New York: Plenum Press.

Stine, S., ed. 1983. *Administration: A Bedside Guide.* Pasadena, CA: Pacific Oaks College.

Stine, S. 1973. *Supporting Change in Public Schools.* Pasadena, CA: Pacific Oaks College.

ACKNOWLEDGMENTS

I'm reminded of a family album, organized photos of people who shared with us special celebrations, trips, and events in our lives. Images of places we enjoyed, found inspiring, or simply wanted to remember. What happened, where, with whom are memories marked by a camera lens, images later placed on pages to be savored and shared.

This acknowledgment is similar to an album of photos that recognizes people and places that have contributed to my work. The 1970 images are of a setting at California Polytechnic State University in San Luis Obispo, where design and early childhood education students worked with me to create, build, and conduct research in a lab school program for five-year-olds. In the 1980s, the snapshots include children at Pacific Oaks College and Children's school and the outside yards. As that campus, its buildings, and grounds approach a one-hundredth birthday, I hope this particular place will be cherished and there to nurture large and small folks for another hundred years.

Turning to the current photos in my album, I see the graduate and undergraduate students in the College of Environmental Design at California State Polytechnic University in Pomona. Their work and commitment to a community design process is an invaluable resource as we explored together the human factors in design. A special page of appreciation to Jim Holas (BSLA 1996), who creatively and carefully produced the 11 plan-view case study site drawings for this book.

There have been many journeys beyond my work setting where I watched, wrote, and wondered about outdoor environments for children and youth. Both people and place have supported my process. Prue Walsch in Australia, thanks for stimulating my thinking as I began research at Pacific Oaks. To the teachers at the American School in Stuttgart, Germany, I appreciate your openness to my visits and my incessant camera clicking. I am grateful to the outdoor cafes, my creative spaces, especially in Spain, where I lingered for hours over one coffee while writing my journal, and to the many people and places in Japan that helped me question the familiar. I am deeply indebted to Otani College faculty and president Takeshi Kuwakado for their patience and understanding of my "American" questions. The current help provided by IPA members in Japan, especially Hiroko Naito, has been invaluable.

This book would not have been possible without the generous support of designers and teachers who shared experiences with me as they told or wrote their stories that appear as case studies in this book: at the Santa Fe Children's Museum—Londi Carabal and Jeff Harner; Tufenkian Armenian School—Ida Karayan; Sonshine School—Mary Taylor; Pacific Oaks Children's School—Julie DeKonig and Frank Sata; Walden School—Carol Per Lee; Rosemead High School—Dan Morris; Midland School—Dan Kunkle; Pacific Oaks Art Studio—Karen Neubert; Lincoln Elementary School— Amaury Rodriguez and Paul Alderson; Kyushu Otani Yochien—Mary Beth Lakin; Coton Community School—Ruth Poulton. Working with all of you has been an inspiring experience.

There are many others whose work has deeply influenced my thinking. The chapter introductions represent some of these people: Mark Francis, professor, Landscape Architecture, University of California–Davis; Elizabeth Jones, professor, Early Childhood Education/Teacher Training, Pacific Oaks College; Carolyn Francis, doctoral candidate in Social and Cultural Factors in Architecture, University of California–Berkeley; Catherine Loughlin and Joseph Suina, professors, Elementary Education/General Elementary Curriculum, University of New Mexico; Ken Nakaba, professor, Landscape Architecture, California State Polytechnic University–Pomona; Elizabeth Prescott, professor emeritus, Pacific Oaks College; John Lyle, professor, Landscape Architecture, California State Polytechnic University–Pomona. I appreciate the many ways your perspective both supports and challenges my ideas. Thank you for your involvement and for introducing the chapters with your stories.

Three people have been with me on this journey, reading drafts of my work and providing invaluable guidance and support. I especially want to thank Elizabeth Jones, Elizabeth Prescott, and Mary Taylor longtime friends and colleagues who encouraged this book and reminded me to be playful.

Finally, this album of acknowledgment is filled with snapshots of my own family: my husband whose faith in my work never wavered and whose willingness to listen to my ideas seemed boundless, our children and grand-children, all children and grandchildren, who touch and enrich my learning and living. This story I've told is yours.

I

◇ ◇

THE PLAYERS

INTRODUCTION

Making places for children and youth must be a participatory process involving many people. It is fundamentally a pro-active process where children, teachers, managers, planners, and designers must all work toward a shared vision of the future—a common image of what makes a good place. In this book, Sharon Stine clearly shows how designers can create a better fit between kids and their environment. She tells teachers and school decision makers how they can be active participants in this process. She also presents practical ways that children and youth can directly participate in the design and planning of outdoor places they use. Most important, Landscapes for Learning should inspire the creation of more engaging, exciting, and meaningful places for children and youth.

—MARK FRANCIS

If I were to build with children in mind, a house would be all attic and eaves, huge closets and little doors, cubbies and alcoves and dark shadowy places, laundry chutes, dumb waiters, settings for mystery and exploration.

—Bartlett 1990, p. 3

Children

As adults, we can all remember those special places we enjoyed during our childhood, places that were significant because we loved to play there: the vacant lot with tall weeds, dirt, and rocks; the space behind the basement heater with pillows and rug scraps; an alleyway or attic filled with shadowy treasures. They were places where plastic horses went on endless journeys complete with aluminum foil saddles that shone in the sun like real silver, or where an orange crate dollhouse had a tiny matchbox bed with the most beautiful red velvet cover. In these child-created worlds we experimented with power and control. Whether in miniature with plastic horses or in a full-size outdoor hideaway, making and exploring special places is an empowering kind of play that seems to be a common experience for children of all cultures (Sobel 1990). Messing about in special places is more than "just fun"; it is how children learn about the world and their place in it (Cobb 1959).

Although children experience a sense of power in their specially created environments, they spend a majority of time in spaces over which they have no control. For example, car trips are vacation activities that are endured by children. The adult looks out a car window and finds enjoyment in the distant views. Passive visual experience does not match a child's active way of being in the world. The child seeks direct sensory stimuli, especially in the out-of-doors.

That adult's-enjoyed view of distant trees, grass, and lake must become a tactile, auditory, oral and olfactory experience for the child. It is through body contact, direct and often disorderly, that children need to experience their world. The adult-avoided mud puddle is a place to experiment with splashing. The adult's vista of a lush green hillside is for a child a place to roll down, feel the wet soft grass, smell its green smell, experience the free fall of tumbling round and round. The outside space for adults is typically dominated by the clean beauty of the visual, not the messy disorder of mud and wet grass. Children as players in the environment are "place-messers."

3

Children playing in a pond is a direct, sensory, often messy experience.

Teachers

> ✦*All of us, to a degree, are designers and environmental engineers. We design our bedrooms, our kitchens, our work spaces . . . as places to crash after a hard day, to focus attention on photographs or art work, . . . as areas to minimize effort . . . We begin with what we want, the lives we want to lead, and apply our resources as best we can.*
>
> —Greenman 1988, p. 22

As that mud-puddle-splashing child tumbles down the grassy hill, the teacher may delight in observing her joyful play while, at the same time, worrying about the problem of clean clothes and appearances. Teachers are often caught between an understanding of how children learn through mess, disorder, and direct sensory contact, and their expectations that somehow learning is neat, organized, and orderly.

Teaching is a profession that has been dominated by females, especially in early childhood education. Adults clean, arrange, and decorate the school or childcare environment in the same way females have traditionally cleaned, maintained, and arranged the home. The architect or landscape architect designs it; the builder builds it; the child explores it; the teacher decorates, arranges, and takes care of it.

Educators often use as arrangement guides curriculum areas such as math, art, science, reading, and so forth, or developmental goals such as

Teachers, using boxes, tires, and boards shape the outside space for children.

socialization, physical development, cognitive thinking, and so on. But the inside environment is more than a room with arrangements of furniture or collections of decorated curriculum areas, and the outside environment is more than a swing, slide, and sand area. A teacher can be more than the arranger and maintainer of the environment.

The teacher has an important role, that of constantly shaping the physical space, both indoors and outside, and this space helps to shape the child's learning. Teachers' thought and decision making in regard to their environments is critical to the entire process of teaching and learning (Loughlin and Suina 1982). Their charge goes beyond the type of tables, the number of chairs, the color of the rugs, the art work on bulletin boards and the selection of play structures. It involves the arrangement of the whole environment as something that significantly influences those who occupy it. It asks the teacher as designer to recognize the relationship between environment and behavior. It asks the designer as teacher to understand the importance of process rather than to focus on a final product.

> ✦*Our attempts to design child-rearing spaces have, for the most part, been too narrow and timid. We think about climbing structures and child-sized furniture, but we do not think about the total child-rearing environment and its ultimate purpose. We must keep in mind that it is not only a place of continuity and stability for children but also a place wherein adults can remember the enchantments of childhood.*
> —Prescott 1987, p. 87

Designers

Teachers, like parents, are often overwhelmed by the complexity of the day-to-day tasks needed to nurture children such as arranging and maintaining space, planning daily experiences, and simply keeping track. The designer, like a supportive grandparent, is in a unique position to offer understanding, past experiences, wisdom, and neutrality to help solve problems. Grandparents' time with their families and their chances to offer support are often limited. For designers, time is also a luxury, yet it takes time for the designer to watch, enjoy, and understand the mud-splashing mess-making child. It takes time for the designer to become sufficiently immersed in a place to understand its purpose directly from the users rather than from abstractions or the stereotypes of children they may hold.

It is difficult for the designer to know clients intimately. Unlike grandparents, designers do not have the wealth of family history to draw upon,

Designer working with teens to develop new images for their school plaza.

that familiar knowledge of sons and daughters from birth. Designers are further distanced from understanding clients because projects are often large, overwhelming in the kinds of decisions that must be made and the complex technologies and regulations that impact a setting. Intimate knowledge is especially difficult in outside play areas because even though children are the primary users, their needs are usually interpreted through adults. Whereas grandparents may share their grandchild's discovery of a worm in the fresh garden soil, the designer seldom has the time or opportunity to learn directly from a child's joyful experience.

As designers engage in a process of developing an image, representing it, and then testing their ideas, they can help teachers as decision makers to become aware of alternative perspectives. They provide a catalyst for change, for achieving an outcome, and, most important, for facilitating a thinking process. In a thoughtful process, the designer takes into account what exists and provides an opportunity for the players to express themselves, to be effective, and to feel empowered. The designer's role is a critical part of the triangle of players who together create a place that goes beyond the narrow and timid to encompass the "enchantments of childhood."

Interactions

✦*Most people who care about child development know nothing about design, and most people who design know nothing about child development.*

—Hart, in Shell 1994, p. 81

Many creative tasks are left to those we label as "talented," those we endow with special qualities while perceiving ourselves as incompetent in a particular area. Artists, singers, and composers embody our notion of creativity among the gifted few; designers also inhabit this special arena in the minds of many. The creation of an environment may be viewed as so special and so difficult that only those with training and talent can design settings (Nicholson 1971). The use of particular tools—drafting table, T-square, vellum—and the language that accompanies the design process—rendering, 30 scale, site conditions—serve to strengthen the barriers to communication between designer and teacher.

People who work directly with children often feel incompetent to experiment, to play around with the components and variables that are a part of the creative process of making spaces for children. "Designers have all the fun with their own materials, concepts and planning alternatives and then builders have all the fun building the environments out of real materials" (Nicholson 1971, p. 30). This is a limiting relationship for all adults engaged in the creation of settings.

The unfortunate outcome of this kind of relationship is that the rich problem-solving process between disciplines is left untried, unexplored. Teachers are often frustrated and designers baffled. For example, when a group of teachers planned the renovation of a preschool outside space, designers spent weeks interviewing staff, observing children, and gathering information. They had an office on campus, inviting comments and involvement with teachers. Meetings were held to generate ideas, plans were drawn, models made. One of the first construction projects was a storage shed with an adjacent swing. A small model was made of this section of the yard. Teachers looked at the model and unanimously approved the design. They were excited about the proposed physical changes to the environment until construction began. Then they stormed into the director's office demanding that construction be stopped and the now-completed storage shed be removed. Their comments included "I didn't know it would be that big and look like that, it blocks my view of the swings . . . We just can't have it there or that high." The designer was confused by the dissatisfaction and complaints: "I showed them drawings, listened to what they needed, even made a small model that the staff OK'd." Somehow a communication process which had included watching children and talking to teachers, failed. No one seemed to be able to reach beyond the basic information that the players provided each other and create a vision for a place that fit the users.

A better understanding of the place-making process is needed. A designer as place maker has a brief but often intense relationship to the environment. As he or she works to guide a fit between users and their space, the designer is in a fleeting, creative, but also powerful, position. Although designers must be concerned with how children will mess about in what they create, with how teachers will maintain the environment, these are future activities. Children and teachers are able to develop a relationship to a place that evolves with use over time. The designer is not. He or she will be viewed by them as someone who came, made an impact, and left. The work of the designer is often seen as a past action difficult to change.

The teacher as a place maintainer is trained in regulating a space for safety and learning. Maintaining and arranging space is a never-ending daily activity. Teachers inherit the consequences of a designer's fleeting creative involvement. When the result—the space—meets the needs of the people who use it, it will have meaning for them, even though the meaning for the child will differ from the meaning for the teacher. This relationship, in which the setting and behavior support each other, or "fit," is often difficult to achieve.

The child seeks rich, sensory stimulation and looks for opportunities to manipulate or mess about in the setting. Unlike the designer, who is viewed as a past player, or the teacher, who must think about future issues, the child is completely focused on the now, the active present.

Conclusion

The three players in creation of a setting, the maker, the maintainer, and the messer, are approaching from different viewpoints, operating at different points in time that are potentially in conflict with each other. The mess and disorder currently being created by the playful child may drive the teacher and the visually trained designer to distraction (Olwig 1990). The adult's emphasis on future issues of appearance may severely limit the child's opportunity to actively explore within the setting. The application of the historical gender stereotype—of cleaning and maintaining a home—to females limits teachers' creative design ideas. The thinking and concepts of a past design process may be lost and no longer available as a catalyst for currently needed physical changes. These three players are discrete parts of a whole, operating within different but overlapping time frames. Like a component of an ecosystem, they must be interrelated but also have lives of their own. Each player's diversity of thought, action, role, skills, and viewpoint should enhance the others' experiences. At times, they will be in conflict, but through an understanding of the different roles, values, and expectations, better collaboration and, ultimately, solutions to the creation of outdoor educational settings for children is possible.

The stories, analytical tools, case histories, and results of research presented in the following chapters focus on questions that stimulate awareness of each of these players, their needs, and their impact on each other in the creation of outside educational settings. How does the planning and creating of environments for children offer adults opportunities to learn through problem solving environment/behavior issues? How can we support teachers' analytical thinking opportunities to test their ideas in action and to see the results in the person/environment behavior interaction? How can the process of creating outdoor educational settings facilitate a productive teaching/learning environment in which teachers are also "thrivers"? Is there a common language, and what is "basic" in an outside play environment for children and adults?

References

Bartlett, Sheridan. 1990. "Introduction." *Children's Environments Quarterly* 7(4):3.

Cobb, Elizabeth. 1959. *The Ecology of Imagination in Childhood.* New York: Columbia University Press.

Greenman, Jim. 1988. *Caring Spaces, Learning Places: Children's Environments That Work.* Redmond, WA: Exchange Press. Published by Child Care Information Exchange, P.O. Box 2890, Redmond, WA, 98073

Loughlin, Catherine, and Joseph Suina. 1982. *The Learning Environment,* New York: Teachers College Press.

Nicholson, Simon. 1971. "How not to cheat children, the theory of loose parts." *Landscape Architecture* 62(1): 30–34.

Olwig, Kenneth R. 1990. "Designs upon children's special places." *Children's Environment Quarterly* 7(4): 47–53.

Prescott, Elizabeth. 1987. "The environment as organizer of intent in child-care settings." In *Spaces for Children: The Built Environment and Child Development*, edited by Carol Weinstein and Thomas David. New York: Plenum Press.

Shell, Ellen Ruppel. 1994. "Kids don't need equipment, they need opportunity." *Smithsonian* 25(4): 79–86.

Sobel, David. 1990. "Favorite places of Estonian adolescents." *Children's Environments Quarterly* 7(4): 32–36.

2

$\diamond \diamond$

BASICS

INTRODUCTION

There were spontaneously gathered groups of three- to five-year-olds all over the large tree-shaded space. Some of them had chosen to dig, rake or pour water in the sand, where teaching staff had provided a variety of gardening tools (and children had added dinosaurs). Several were keeping house, with dolls and dishes, in the space defined by a low railed platform. Three had invented a chasing-and-catching drama in another corner. The heart of the action was an area defined by boulders and pebbles, a bit of grass and plenty of dirt, rosemary bushes, and a small stream bed where adults had provided trowels, a tub of water with containers for scooping and pouring, and a worm bin. "Can anyone find a worm?" a teacher asked. For nearly an hour eight to ten children happily and peacefully explored the dirt and rocks, created a stream, and discovered worms, pill bugs, ants, roots, and some of those special rocks that really need to be taken home and cherished.

Because children are highly motivated to learn about everything, effective teachers of the very young manipulate environments, not children. Designers and teachers set the stage for children's learning about their bodies and what they can do, their relationships with other people, and all the wonders of the world.

—ELIZABETH JONES

Through play, children (and bigger people, too) learn a great deal about the variety and complexity of the world, and about themselves as self-directed learners.

—Jones and Prescott 1978, p. 1

Play

◆*Play lies at the heart of childhood, limited in its boundaries only by the opportunities afforded by physical settings and by the attitudes and commitment of those whose business it is to manage them.*

—Moore 1990, p. 18

Dancing in public space is playful social learning in Germany.

The outside space as an educational setting for children is often neglected (Francis 1990) or viewed as something left over (Cohen, McGinty, and Moore 1978). There is "little in the literature on day care outdoor space and . . . the greatest range of literature on designing learning environments and play areas dates from late 1960s to the mid 1970s." (Francis 1990, p. 218). Yet, in spite of the limited material focusing on children's outside play environments, there are a number of excellent guidelines and design recommendations (Esbensen 1987; Francis 1990; Greenman 1988; Jones 1977; Kritchevsky and Prescott 1969; Moore, Goltsman, and Iacofano 1987; Prescott 1987; Shaw 1987; Titman 1994; Walsh 1988; Weinstein and David 1987). These authors tend to agree, emphasizing similar elements that are essential for the overall quality of space and for children's growth and development. To meet program goals of socialization, cognitive development and physical maturation, authors in both early childhood education and environmental design focus on the importance of facilitation of children's play.

Youth delights in encasing himself in a bubble.

Dramatic kinds of play are part of the way a child learns

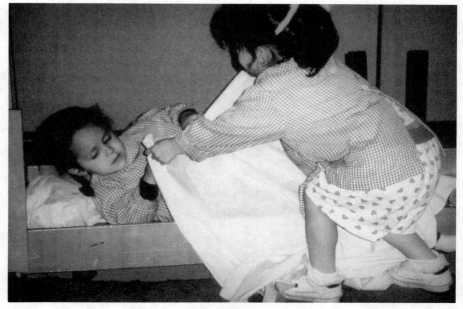

Play as a behavior has generated many definitions, descriptions, and developmental theories. Most frequently, play refers to spontaneous activity that is child initiated and terminated (Moore 1990; Jones and Prescott 1978). Building on the work of many others in the field of social research, I make the following four assumptions. First, play is the way children learn and is an essential part of their growth and development. Second, play is not limited to young children. Adults engage in play as an essential experience throughout the life cycle. Third, playing outside is an intrinsic need because it provides a uniqueness of experience that cannot be offered elsewhere. Finally, play environments are educational settings.

In summary, play can be described in terms of "The Child's Right to Play" :

- *Children have played at all times throughout history and in all cultures.*
- *Play, along with the basic needs of nutrition, health, shelter and education, is vital to develop the potential of all children.*
- *Play is communication and expression, combining thought and action; it gives satisfaction and a feeling of achievement.*
- *Play is instinctive, voluntary and spontaneous.*

Finding a place where they can watch others is important to young people.

- *Play helps children develop physically, mentally, emotionally and socially.*
- *Play is a means of learning to live, not a mere passing of time.*
  —IPA *Declaration of the Child's Right to Play*, revised Barcelona, September 1989

◆*The type, quality and diversity of the physical setting we create for children directly affects the type, quality and diversity of the child's play.*
—Jones and Prescott 1978, p. 43

The physical environment supports play activities through complexity and variety (Kritchevsky and Prescott 1969). These basic classifications have to do with the variety of ways a child is able to use materials—riding, digging, running, building, swinging, painting—and the potential for active manipulation and alternation by the child. Complexity and variety also include

Exploring the environment is an adventure that involves solving problems

richness in social interaction and problem-solving opportunities. If a play environment can be described as complex and providing variety, it should involve and sustain a child's interest over time.

Problem solving opportunities, potential for choice, and sustained interest are all considerations a teacher might describe as important support for children's play behavior (Jones and Reynolds 1992). When these ideas are translated into a built form, there are various interpretations both teachers and designers might make. How things look to different adults, "interesting" or "cute" or "messy" or "clean," is defined by culture, values, training, individual interpretation, and ongoing personal judgment.

Children are "mess makers."

✦*A slide framed by a large, brightly colored elephant cut-out while delightful to the adult eye is still a simple unit to a child. . . . [On the other hand] traditional equipment, "old hat" to adults . . . has perhaps become traditional because it supplies important (and often unique) experiences. . . . Single swings offer something unique to children.*
—Kritchevsky and Prescott 1969, p. 29

In making decisions about what is basic in an outside environment, the difference between what is pleasing to the adult's eye, what "looks good," may, after analysis, fail to provide important play experiences for the child. A slide is for sliding, as any child knows; it is a simple structure with a single purpose. Decorative elephant shapes make no difference to that purpose. A swing, another example of an enduring traditional built form, does not need to be suspended from brightly colored clowns to attract children's interest, use, and enjoyment. What are the elements that cause a swing, this simple structure, to endure over time as basic in outside play environments?

Tradition— In Defense of Swings

✦*When I swing, I close my eyes, I feel higher . . .*
—Smith 1974, p. 138

Although it is generally true that the traditional playground in this country is "an arena of concrete and steel, comprised typically of a jungle gym, merry-go-round, slide, seesaw and swings, all designed and used primarily for one form of play—exercise" (Frost 1985, p. 166), swings offer opportunities much more complex than simply "exercise."

Pumping a swing is a skill that marks a new ability

Swings provide a variety of experiences in trust.

As a physical form, swings offer a particular way of sitting. The sitting experience depends on the type of swing seat: a tire, a knot on a rope, a soft rubber toddler seat, or a board. Regardless of safety issues involved in the type of swing seat, the construction material and the child's body position create certain physical experiences. For some children, the feeling of a form around them, the way it shapes to their bottom and sides, the chains or the rope to hold on to, provide a sense of security and well-being. As this sitting area encompasses the child's body shape, he or she feels safe. Sitting there in that particular shape suspended above the ground, the body has weight and can be propelled through the air.

As the child grows, certain physical skills become landmarks. Balancing a bike without training wheels, being able to catch a ball thrown by another person, pumping a swing are all important learned motor activities. Pumping a swing, in particular, is a rite of passage. It is one of the first things children learn to do out-of-doors whereby they can mark their physical skill: "I wasn't able to do that before, and now I can." Pumping reinforces the child's understanding: *I learned a physical skill that provided me with independence and autonomy.*

✦ *"We're swinging crookeds, crookeds, crookeds . . . "*
—Smith 1974, p. 136

Swings provide particular social experiences with adults and other children. They are nice places to cement a friendship. While swinging adjacent to another child, you don't have to make conversation, and yet often the back-and-forth rhythm inspires the invention of word games. These invented rhymes have their own pattern and meaning and, unlike words used for social purposes, these words can fly off into the air, a shared experience in only sound and motion.

For very young children, swings offer a trust exercise, an experience of trusting adults to be there, to push not too high, too fast, or too hard. Swinging forces adults to respond in a caring way and gives those who might be awkward in caring for children something to do with them that is ultimately familiar. Adults can push a swing and experience success even when they consider themselves "not good with" or lacking experience with young children.

The swing environment can be important at times of transitions. The child's day is often filled with adult-dictated transitions: cleanup time, time to line up to go to lunch, time to get ready for naps, circle time, bathroom time. The child's ability to take time when moving from one activity to another is important. Doing nothing is often neither understood nor valued as a part of a child's decision-making process. Swings are places where a child can "do nothing." They are places to go when an activity is finished. A child can hop on, look over the yard, and make an eventual choice. Swings are places where children are "doing something" in the adult's view, but that "something" may be decision making about where and when to get involved. They are places to observe, to think, to simply "be" without an adult bothering the child about being busy.

Swings can be places to cement a friendship.

There are endless problem-solving activities that can take place in a swing area. With a limited number of places to swing, decisions must be made about who gets to swing, how long and what determines the completion of one child's "turn." These questions can become the subjects of complex negotiations between children, with elaborate rituals created to ensure taking turns or physical control of a particular space.

Basic Design Elements: Finding a Common Vocabulary

Besides swings, there are other things in the environment that children will naturally be attracted to, will use and interact with on their own. It does not take an adult or another child to support engagement in environments that include these elements. Water is a primary example. Whether in the natural environment—a stream, a pond, or the beach—or in an urban setting—a plaza fountain or reflecting pool—water offers endless opportunities to explore. It attracts children of all ages to act, to find out what happens if. . . . Boxes, blankets, and pillows also seem to invite children's use; creating hideaways can be endlessly absorbing. Trikes and bikes invite motion, a physical challenge different from the exploratory lure of water or the fort-building appeal of a box and a blanket. These vehicles challenge physical ability, motion, coordination, balance, and testing skills.

Water, boxes and trikes are examples of materials that invite children's play activities. The setting including the "attracting" materials can be ana-

Play frequently involves challenges and risks.

lyzed for cues to aid in the creation of play spaces for children. Such cues are not limited to single or specific features but describe a range of basic dimensions, essential qualities of play spaces, that support the needs and activities of children.

The following nine dimensions are tools that can be used to assess and change outside play environments. Both elements in each of the pairs are needed and used like a check list. The contrasting pairs can help build a space. Each element in itself is neither positive nor negative. They all are essential in the creation of outdoor settings offering guidance in meeting the needs of children intellectually, socially, cognitively, and physically. The pairs of contrasting words described in this section are applied to children and their opportunities to learn through play activities. In Chapter 6, "Back to Basics" these dimensions are applied to teachers and their needs for variety, challenge, and relaxation. The descriptive elements are the basis of a language that can provide design guidelines for both groups of players as they determine how to facilitate children's play in outside settings.

Accessible and Inaccessible Confusion is the result when an environment does not provide cues about what is accessible and what isn't. Concentrating on access issues directs time and energy away from the facilitation of play activities. Children spend time learning what they can't touch or should get into. Adults spend time "policing" the setting. The teacher is in the position to limit children's activities and choice by creating physical inaccessibility or to promote independence and participation through accessibility of materials.

Because of their size, children find the world accessible and inaccessible differently from adults. Their view is not ours. They are limited in what they can reach, see, touch, and, thus, explore. The inaccessibility of certain areas, materials, and views because of the child's size, is important to recognize, as both negative—a learning limitation—and positive—a clarity and safety provision. For example, if a child cannot see the possibilities for play activities or reach an area (i.e., a sink) he or she cannot explore the learning opportunity available there. Inaccessibility clarifies the environment and makes it possible to limit what is available to a child.

Because children are close to the ground, this is an accessible area to them, and changing the ground surfaces has an impact on their play. As packed dirt becomes soft sand and then wet grass, children play differently on these ground coverings. Differences in surfaces can define and clarify potential activities. On the other hand, elevation, seeing things by looking down on them, is a vantage point usually not accessible to children. By

These doves and their newborn are inaccessible, for viewing only from a stool.

making it available, we allow children to see their world in another way. A small mound or bridge a child can climb, a gully or deck a child can be under or within, invite exploration of areas accessible—(ground level), and previously inaccessible—(elevation).

Active and Passive We tend to think of inside spaces as quiet places, environments where we sit and engage in small-muscle activities. An outside area is frequently seen as a place where children can be physically active as they loudly participate in large-muscle activity. Outside noise is permitted; inside it usually is not. Yet being out of doors does not mean that children should or want to engage in vigorous, active play. Adults frequently seek an outdoor setting for the peaceful, relaxing, calm, meditative, passive quality it provides. For young people too an outside area can be a place to relax, to dream, to enjoy the sky and space. Lying on your back, watching the shapes of clouds, the pattern of light through the leaves, can only be done outside. The outdoors should be a place where both active and passive activities occur.

*Low sinks step down in height
and are accessible to toddlers.*

*Active noisy play is usually
allowed outdoors.*

Children need to be able to retreat to quiet, passive places outside.

Providing both active and passive potential in outside environments causes us to think about the "edges." Where does the potential for one activity end and another begin? If children run, jump, scream, throw balls in this space, what is the impact on a private retreat nearby? Figuring out ways children can choose their own kind of mobility, active or passive, without compromising the quality of either, is a difficult issue. It means that "letting off steam" is only one choice, rather than the expected play behavior, in an outdoor setting.

Challenge/Risk and Repetition/Security

Humans represent a range of physical abilities. We are all somewhere on a continuum of high to low physical abilities and, therefore, enjoy watching others test the upper limits. Physical challenges also mean physical risks. In a reading or writing environment, such as a school library, materials represent a wide range of skill levels without any risk to a person's safety. On the other hand, a challenging physical environment supporting multiple competence levels is potentially dangerous for some young people. A child who is able to read has a choice of books at many different levels and can explore and test his cognitive skill. A child who is able to climb and balance her body needs different levels that she can explore to safely test her physical skill. What is challenging for one child may be a hazard for another because of the developmental range of skills and abilities.

And yet, by taking risks, by facing a challenge, we learn about our competence and our limitations. Trying to exist in a world without some

Jumping off boxes provides a challenge.

measure of risk is not only impossible but inhibits our lives and denies a child's need for challenge (Walsh 1988). It is important for children to be able to risk without physical danger. If there is an absence of risk for children, they will often use their own initiative to create their own challenges, seeking stimulation in ways that may endanger their safety. There must be protection and safeguards against injury so that children are not confronted with challenges they are unable to meet.

Repeating an activity or doing it with another person gives a feeling of security

Children also need to be able to repeat an activity many times as a way of practicing a growing competence when it is no longer a challenging risk. There is an element of comfort and security in repetition. That first time down a slide may represent a risk and a challenge; however, sliding becomes an activity that is joyously repeated and practiced over time. Walking along on a low wall is initially a risk and challenge to a child's balancing ability, yet it continues to be a chosen pathway that is repeatedly traversed for years after the initial challenge. Predictable security is an essential element in building self-confidence; taking risks within limits of safety is important to a child's learning through active play.

Hard and Soft Children touch their physical world using their entire bodies, and that environment responds to their touch. Wet mud squishes through toes, a metal slide imprints its smooth surface on legs, a kitten's fur tickles the fingertips. When an environment gives way under the body's touch, when our senses respond to that feeling of giving, the environment seems "soft." Thick pile rugs, mats of grass, fluffy down pillows, furry rabbits, the edge of the beach where the ocean meets the sand, all physical forms that respond to touch, are examples of the quality of softness found in our physical environment.

Bubbles and grass provide a soft way to play.

Hard spaces support wheel toy activities.

On the other hand, hardness provides opportunities for activities that need a nongiving surface or require cleanliness and ease of maintenance. Cooking activities, painting, stacking blocks, and propelling wheel toys are all activities that must take place on tables, cement, tile, or other hard-surfaced areas. However, if an environment becomes primarily hard, designed to be resistant to human imprint, it appears impersonal to those who use it. Such settings become easier to maintain but are less responsive to the overall needs of children (Jones 1977).

Natural and People Built As our society becomes increasingly technological, it gets more difficult to understand how something is built by taking it apart. Many of today's products are impervious to exploration. In the past, when a child watched things being built or repaired, the process was a part of the resulting product. The child who collects and treasures a motorcycle part found along the street may fantasize about having the complete machine after finding just enough pieces. The found treasure indicates possibilities, and the process seems possible when children are connected to people who can be watched building things. It is difficult to create if we don't have the chance to "tinker" with objects, to experience things being made, to see and learn the process and its connection to materials.

An important part of our foundation, formed in the natural world, is also removed as we become more isolated from rural life processes. Children don't see how crops grow, how animals complete their cycle of life. These limitations are barriers to experiencing the wonders of the natural world, its changes and conversions. Going to the store to buy products, neatly and sanitarily packaged for consumption, becomes the child's understanding of crops. Cooking the store-purchased foods and witnessing the changes resulting from heating is perhaps the closest they get to the change process in natural materials.

Without exposure to a range of activities in the natural world, children's play and learning experiences are restricted. Interaction with plant and animal materials such as smooth stones, rough bark, wet fur, fuzzy leaves, and soft feathers provide sensory experiences different from those offered

Growing vegetables helps children touch their natural world.

By jumping on this water-squirting piston, a child can explore a people-made object.

by a manufactured tricycle or metal slide. People- built elements are a part of our culture and represent ways that humans solve complex problems. To learn about, to value, and to ultimately protect their world, children need to experience it fully in both its natural and built forms, where process is interwoven with product.

Open and Closed Open activities provide an opportunity to explore, to create, to become enchanted by the process without any consideration for an end product. A sand area, dress-up corner, water table, and painting easel are all potential places for open-ended play. When a painting activity takes place on a clear plexiglass easel, from which the paint is washed off when the child is finished, there is no resulting product or picture to take home. The art activity is process driven. These types of activities that lack a particular goal or defined end product can be described as open. In open environments children are able to make their own choices from a variety of alternatives without product constraints.

Painting on Plexiglas is a process, an open activity.

Games with rules are closed activities.

Close-ended activities provide feedback, showing that we have successfully completed, correctly solved, or produced a product. Puzzles, a basketball and hoop, and video games (when played by the rules) are all examples of closed-play activities. When a puzzle piece is carefully placed in a pattern of potential spaces, the child learns immediately whether it fits, whether this is the correct place. With success comes a feeling of accomplishment and closure.

Open activities foster exploration and discovery, whereas a closed activity helps develop self-esteem based on competence. The child knows when he or she is successful with closed activities through the feedback provided by the end result. The physical environment can be designed to support both open-ended discovery, such as play with water or sand, and closed-ended product completion activities, such as ball games with rules.

Permanence and Change When we change something, we clarify a question for ourselves; making changes is a way we think and solve problems. We also have routines, which in their repetition and permanence, give meaning and structure to our lives.

> ◆*The same children would come by the office daily, to pet Paz [school cat]. It was their special ritual, the way they began and ended their school day. Even when he wasn't in his basket at the time, children asked, and were comforted to know . . . Paz is eating in the kitchen, in Adventure Yard with the children, sleeping in the Parent Lounge.*
>
> —Dean's Notes, Pacific Oaks, 1984

We carry with us visual images of landmarks in our neighborhoods, schools, and towns that are permanent reminders of a sense of place. A church spire, a fishing bridge, or a tree might mark the area a person calls "my home" or "my school." Landmarks are elements that stand out strongly against their backgrounds and help establish the identity of place (Lynch, 1960). We carry those images with us; they help us know where we are, and we invest them with feelings about how important a place is in our life (Hart 1979).

This school drinking fountain is a permanent landmark for the children.

Children also need the permanence of landmarks in their school setting to provide strong visual clues that this is a special place. The permanence of a landmark and its imprint as a clear memory of a particular environment can help children develop physiological independence (Moore et al. 1987). That landmark helps children to know where they are, negotiate where they are going, and organize their pathways of exploration. A child can venture forth, secure in the knowledge that "I'll find my way, I'm safe." The challenge is to discover the kind of permanence that is effective in helping a child orient him- or herself. A landmark, such as the school cat in its basket on the office desk, becomes more powerful because a child can interact with it. A drinking fountain where runoff waters a mulberry tree is a familiar place to pause, to drink, to watch the water splash down the rocks. To the child this is a permanent landmark, a daily place to pause and use, that says, "my school is here."

We clarify concepts for ourselves when we change something physically. When a group of teachers were upset with the size and location of a storage shed, they understood the importance of scale and views. Even though these same teachers had been involved in the planning and design and had approved the drawings and the scale model of this outside structure, it wasn't until it was actually built, when that area of the yard changed physically, that they clearly understood their priorities. Teachers need to change their

Boards and boxes can be changed to provide flexibility in a play space.

environment to think through their goals, to test ideas in action, and to see the results. Flexibility in a space, in contrast to the permanence of landmarks, means that we can experiment. This stimulates thinking about what might work, what didn't work, and what should be changed. Children need to be a part of changing the space. Their actions on the environment have consequences; they learn about these consequences by active involvement. When an environment cannot be physically changed or rearranged, everyone loses opportunities for growth and creative problem solving.

Private and Public In settings where young people spend long days together, they need opportunities to choose when to be with people and when to be alone or with a special friend. When children can make these choices and thus regulate the rhythm of their social relationships, they are better able to engage in playful activities (Prescott 1987).

Privacy has to do with boundaries and who or what comes through them. Each boundary may be more or less permeable through sensory perception: visual, auditory, tactile, and olfactory. If any type of stimulation invades our sense of privacy, it lessens our feelings of control over our space: taped music overwhelms the sound of waves at a beach; graffiti dominates freeway signs; cigar smoke lingers at empty tables in an outdoor cafe. The fulfillment of

Building a barrier of tires creates privacy, a place to be alone.

some of our basic human needs for identity and security is linked to our ability to preserve privacy through control of the environment (Lang 1974).

Because we must create safe environments for children, teachers exercise a great deal of control over the amount of privacy allowed. A playhouse can be built with abundant open areas enabling teachers to see inside. A cardboard box is a safe playhouse because of its open end. Like adults, children need to have some sense of seclusion during their day, places to withdraw from social interaction, spaces to think private thoughts. What extent does a physical setting permit children to be alone, in small groups, or part of a large group?

Young people are also a part of unique communities. There are times when being in a larger group means giving up privacy and control over space. Group gatherings help youth understand their place as individuals within the whole. These are occasions when the setting must allow all types of physical, visual, auditory, and even olfactory intrusion. The ability to arrange spaces to accommodate group gatherings is important in both the inside and outside environment.

Gathering for a school sing is a shared activity that builds community.

Simple and Complex Simple units, such as a slide, a swing, or a tricycle have one obvious use. The materials encourage one type of activity and do not enable a child to manipulate or improvise. Complex environments are those to which additional elements have been added, such as placing buckets of soapy water and sponges in a trike area. With these added elements the space becomes a car wash where different roles may be played. When an area has more than one type of material with one obvious use, and allows the child to manipulate or change it in some way, it is a complex area (Kritchevsky and Prescott 1969). Making choices about swinging, digging in the sand, or painting depends on the materials available and how the environment is set up for a child. When a water table is set next to a large window area and soap bubbles, paint, brushes and kitchen basters are added, the window becomes an easel for painting or a place to experiment in projecting soapy water, or a site for a combination of activities. The choices as to what to do in this area are complex because of the many different materials that may be used together.

A major problem in choice making is that there is often not enough to choose from, not enough to do! Adding complexity is one way to provide more choices for children. For example, with the addition of small dinosaurs and colored water to a sand table, the child is able to manipulate and improvise endless activities.

Simple play areas provide structure and direction. Adding complexity encourages children to make choices and play in unpredictable ways. If we want to provide children with spaces and activities to better meet their individual needs and to facilitate their learning through play, creating both simple and complex environments is important.

Games with one obvious use are simple units.

A water table, bubbles, paints, and a window to paint on make up a complex area.

CHILDREN'S PLAY ACTIVITY SPACE NEEDS
Basic Design Elements

Accessible	Inaccessible
Active	Passive
Challenge/Risk	Repetition/Security
Hard	Soft
Natural	People-Built
Open	Closed
Permanence	Change
Private	Public
Simple	Complex

Basic design dimensions in outside spaces for children.

Conclusion   ✦*Kids don't need equipment, they need opportunity.*
                                                        —Shell 1994, p. 79

The basic design elements summarized in the preceding chart can be used as a guide to evaluate and change an outside play environment. These dimensions are neither positive nor negative, simply contrasting; all are important in designing an outside space as a place where creative play is valued as fulfilling a vital need during childhood. The elements offer a common language for designers and teachers in working together to change the landscape of childhood so that children's imagination can truly take over.

All environments work for us or against us in some way (Hall 1969). In considering quality of life, we may ask the basic question, "What does it feel like to live and work at a certain place day after day?" (Greenman 1988). What does it take for a child to play outside? The decision is not unlike choosing an outdoor cafe table. When walking along a sidewalk on a warm evening looking for a place to pause, an adult makes many decisions in that seemingly simple act of sitting at a cafe. Is there a place where it's cool, shady, or warm, with a breeze? Is there a view of the passing crowd? Is it too near traffic noise, or is someone smoking a cigar nearby? What beverages are offered, what are the food choices? Can I sit alone and enjoy privacy? Is there enough space for others to join me if I move some chairs? Will I be able to read here, to write or sketch, to talk? Adults make these decisions related to their perception of a physical space and their assessment of its potential use. We make a choice, based on our evaluation of the absence or presence of many elements which are not limited simply to furnishings. This is a complex decision, made in a short period of time.

For the child going outside to play, decision making is also complex. Like the cafe furnishings, play structures support only a limited number of activities. There may be variety in the ways a child can physically move on a structure, but the complexity of children's needs and behaviors are not addressed by this single built form. Unfortunately, play structure decisions often become the dominant focus of outside space planning (Prescott 1986). Instead an outside space needs to be analyzed according to the presence or absence of a range of dimensions. An area with trees where the leaf litter can be incorporated into sand play, or with boards, boxes, and ladders that become child-created structures, or with a combination of cement, grass, dirt, and water, can support a variety of play activities.

When used as an analytical tool by both teachers and designers, these nine pairs of elements help the players avoid a limited vision, relying on the addition of a structure to solve an issue of outdoor play space design. These dimensions can help teachers and designers clarify what is missing, as well as what is offered by a particular environment, and then together envision inventive solutions that provide children a wider range of possible activities and opportunities to learn through play.

References

Cohen, Uriel, Tim McGinty, and Gary T. Moore. 1978. *Case Studies of Child Play Areas and Child Support Facilities.* WI: Center for Architecture and Urban Planning Research, University of Wisconsin Press, Milwaukee.

Esbensen, Steen. 1987. *An Outdoor Classroom.* MI: High Scope Press.

Francis, Carolyn. 1990. "Day care outdoor spaces." In *People Places: Design guidelines for Urban Open Space,* edited by C. Cooper Marcus and C. Francis. New York: Van Nostrand Reinhold.

Frost, Joe L. 1985. "The American playground movement." In *When Children Play,* edited by J. L. Frost and S. Sunderlin. MD: Association for Childhood Education International.

Greenman, Jim. 1988. *Caring Spaces, Learning Places: Children's Environments That Work.* Redmond, WA: Exchange Press.

Hall, E. T. 1969. *The Hidden Dimension.* New York: Doubleday.

Hart, Roger. 1979. *Children's Experience of Place.* New York: Irvington Publishers.

IPA Declaration of the Child's Right to Play, revised by the IPA International Council Barcelona, Sept., 1989, National Play Information Center, London, UK.

Jones, Elizabeth. 1977. *Dimensions of Teaching-Learning Environments: Handbook for Teachers.* Pasadena, CA: Pacific Oaks College.

Jones, Elizabeth and Elizabeth Prescott. 1978. *Dimensions of Teaching Learning Environments II. Focus on Day Care.* Pasadena CA: Pacific Oaks College.

Jones, Elizabeth and Gretchen Reynolds. 1992. *The Play's the Thing: Teachers' Roles in Children's Play.* New York: Teachers College Press.

Kritchevsky, Sybil and Elizabeth Prescott. 1969. *Planning Environments for Young Children: Physical Space.* Washington, DC: National Association for the Education of Young Children.

Lang, Jon. 1987. *Creating Architectural Theory: The Role of the Behavioral Scientist in Environmental Design.* New York: Van Nostrand Reinhold.

Lynch, Kevin. 1960. *The Image of the City.* Cambridge, MA: The MIT Press.

Moore, Robin. 1990. *Childhood's Domain: Play and Place in Child Development.* Berkeley, CA: MIG Communications.

Moore, Robin, Susan Goltsman, and Daniel Iacofano, eds. 1987. *Play for All Guidelines.* Berkeley, CA: MIG Communications.

Prescott, Elizabeth. 1987. "The environment as organizer of intent in child-care settings." In *Spaces for Children: The Built Environment and Child Development*, edited by C. Weinstein and T. David. New York: Plenum.

Shaw, Leland G. 1987. "Designing playgrounds for able and disabled children." In *Spaces for Children: The Built Environment and Child Development*, edited by C. Weinstein and T. David. New York: Plenum Press.

Shell, Ellen R. 1994. "Kids don't need equipment, they need opportunity." *Smithsonian* 25(4): 79–86.

Smith, Grace. 1974. "On listening to the language of children." *Young Children* (March). Washington, DC: National Association for the Education of Young Children. 133–140.

Titman, Wendy. 1994. *Special Places: Special People.* Surrey, UK: World Wide Fund for Nature/Learning Through Landscapes.

Walsh, Prue. 1988. *Early Childhood Playgrounds.* Watson, Australia: Australian Early Childhood Association.

Weinstein, Carol and Thomas David. 1987. *Spaces for Children: The Built Environment and Child Development.* New York: Plenum Press.

3

✦ ✦

PARTICULAR PLACES: SCHOOL ENVIRONMENTS OVER TIME

INTRODUCTION

The kitchen floor in my great-great-aunt's house sloped down, toward the back of the house. When I was five or so, I thought it was because it made it easier to mop, the sudsy water all conveniently making its way toward the back door, to be swooshed out with an old-fashioned string mop. I also thought it was just a curious fact that instead of any sort of real grass in their back yard, they had sand. But as time went on, my mother shared stories of her childhood, and her own mother's. I began to see the house in new ways.

To get to the ocean used to mean a long walk, across a field, over grassy dunes. Now it was just outside across the sand. There had been a big covered veranda on the front of the house, where people sat outside on warm evenings. Now the old ladies sat inside watching variety shows, a little pro wrestling. The ancient, woody-stemmed rose, all unkempt and wild outside the guest bedroom window, had scratched its thorny, whipping canes against the screen when the wind blew, and my child-mother had cowered under her covers, knowing beyond doubt that a terrifying witch with a warty nose was slowly scraping that dreadful appendage back and forth, contemplating the unthinkable.

That house was full of magic: curious quaint wall paper, toys so old you'd never seen them in stores, big glass jars of candy like those in a corner store, homemade preserves and secret-recipe mincemeat—but more than anything, it was filled with the amiable ghosts of family, people I had never met and never would, generations of children long since grown, all of whom had inhabited the same space I was now in, had sat in some of the chairs, opened the doors, slept and dreamt and maybe, as I did, first counted all the way to one hundred. There is something extraordinary about sharing that place with everyone else, sensing that our experiences of the house, barn, yard, somehow form a multilayered collage through time, a lived experience of the poetry of connection between people and place.

If there is one characteristic which seems to increase the chances that a place will endure, it is the "owning" of the setting by a community. Often, it is the vision and determination of a single individual that leads to the creation of places that are very special. However, it is the involvement of a group of people in caring for and making decisions regarding a place that seems critical to its ability to thrive over time. As designers and stewards of the physical environment, we need to understand and support the conditions which foster the development and sustenance of such places.

—CAROLYN FRANCIS

*We are threatened today by two kinds of environmental
degradation: one is pollution—a menace that we all acknowledge;
the other is loss of meaning. For the first time in human history,
people are systematically building meaningless places.*
—Walter 1988, p. 2.

**Images and Idea
Generation**

The physical environment, home, school, or neighborhood—"place identity"—supports the formation of self-identity during childhood years
(Proshansky and Fabian 1987). Social interactions, acquisition of knowledge,
and understandings of the world are rooted in a child's experiences in the
physical space (Wolfe and Rivlin 1987). Children need to actively explore,
use , gain knowledge of, and develop feelings for places in order to learn.
They invest particular environments with meaning and name them as special
places to be either valued or feared (Hart 1979).

The importance of particular places continues to influence us as adults
when we develop careers, establish values, and determine approaches to life.
The meanings we gain from particular places as adults may inspire work,
serve in supportive ways, and challenge thinking.

> ◆*There is a street in Seville made up of superimposed balconies,
> elevated bridges, stairs, noise and silence, and it seems to recur in all
> my drawings . . . here the search has ended.*
> —Rossi 1981, p. 19.

This sense of attachment and meaning whereby we remember the
smells, colors, and textures of special places and invest these with feelings of
affiliation has been studied by educators and designers (Chawla 1992;
Cooper Marcus 1992; Hester 1985; Moore 1990). For example, Downing
has described the role of place imagery in the life a designer, as follows:

> We all have a stock of memorable spaces and events. They are memorable for various
> personal, aesthetic, and abstract reasons, ranging from adventures in tree houses to
> quiet nights and timeless places. It allows the designer to surpass simplistic copying;
> it endows meaning to the creative act of making PLACES. (1992, p. 65)

47

Like designers, teachers may draw upon memories of place events to inspire work. These images, which are frequently from childhood, may be reminders of what it is like to be a child—sitting close to grandmother, listening to her read a story while gently rocking outside on the porch swing, watching the lights and shadows created by the leaves in the adjacent tree. This remembered event may support the value of reading aloud to children. It may inspire the selection of curriculum material. Yet the memory of physical space may seldom impact a teacher's arrangement of a school environment. The softness of the swing, the texture of the trees, the privacy of the porch remain a pleasurable memory rather than a challenge to make a place for reading that is soft, textured, and private. Teachers' salient memories often seem to be dominated by their pictures of "school."

The physical image of "school" is powerful in its similarity among adults even though their childhood experiences are individual, unique, and diverse. Adults know what school should look like. They have an oversimplified understanding of the history of place based on popular images. This limited knowledge of school form is dominated by the image of a "little red school house" with teacher's desk on a front platform, black slate boards, and benches in rows. The outside space is remembered as a hard surface with some metal play equipment, perhaps a swing. Our school-based stock of memorable places does not offer the same richness or diversity of form as a streetscape in Seville or front porch with grandmother. It is difficult to use our school images to think creatively about physical forms that differ from these historic roots.

The physical features of educational settings for the preschool age child are less clear in our minds. Unlike elementary or high school environments, built for an educational purpose, early childhood settings are often carved out of inherited, hand-me-down, or shared space (Francis 1990). The church basement, the local YMCA gym, and old storefront, a new office complex or shopping mall are all early childhood settings. Even though these physical forms are incredibly varied, there is often a quality of sameness in their space design. When dominated by catalog-purchased materials, early childhood programs become look-alike environments similar to franchised motels. In their sameness, these settings provide predictability, an important quality in a highly mobile society. On the other hand, patterned similarity makes it difficult to personalize the adults who work there or the children who play in the setting. The physical form no longer fills the imagination with stories nor describes why or who. Meaning is missing.

Particular Places

◆*The placemakers lay claim to our memories and, as is often the case, to our affection. They offer an anecdote to humanize the face of much new development, and they can build a sense of future value for neglected older environments. It is a value based on associations and images which convey strongly enough that they imprint themselves on the landscape of the mind. . . . by populating the mind with images . . . its history . . . placemakers help us to restore a feeling of belonging.*

—Flemming and von Tscharner 1981, p. 7–8.

An educational setting can be a "placemaker." A school that remains relatively unchanged over time may communicate a sense of who came before and what is valued in this particular place. The history of such educational settings is carved in their physical form like initials in an old wooden desk. Their founding vision continues to guide current values and practices. Such a school has physical forms that imprint themselves on the landscape of the mind.

◆ *Is it still there—the tree?—I used to teach in the building in the 60s, walk under and around that tree, look up into it, tie ropes so kids could swing on it. I don't know why I came back after all these years, just was in the area on vacation, wanted to see if it is all still here, how it's changed. I think about this place and remember how I taught, what I value.*

—Visitor to Pacific Oaks, 1983

An understanding of the history of a particular place is rich in clues of what worked or didn't work for the adults who, over generations, changed or preserved the physical forms, and for the children who learned by exploring in the setting. Our ancestors used to learn a great deal from storytellers, those whose tales of past events and places helped others gain wisdom, create new visions, or discover ways to solve problems. Today these stories are seldom collected or shared. But it remains important to learn about the creation of a physical environment for children by understanding its history, its process of change over time.

The following are two case studies of educational institutions founded more than 70 years ago that have endured with a special "sense of place." The stories that make up the history of each of these schools describe the interaction among the three groups of players. The outside physical settings have continually been impacted by young people, teachers, and designers. Both schools are located in California and are currently active—one serving young children, the other teenagers. Both were founded by people with a strong vision of the underlying values of the educational program they hoped to develop on a site they chose. What has physically changed, what has been preserved over the years, and why? What environmental problems have teachers encountered? What was the design process over time? What can we learn from these environments simply because they have lasted as educational settings for many generations of players?

EARLY CHILDHOOD ENVIRONMENT CASE STUDY
Broadoaks—An Outdoor Kindergarten and Elementary School, Pasadena, California

The Roots:
Early 1900s

◆ *This site near the arroyo had beautiful oaks, one of them hundreds of years old. It was reached by a path through the grain fields. During the building of the house, the sisters supervised its erection with great care for the majestic old oak that became almost a part of the structure. The stairway curving down around its trunk from the second story was later to become the path taken by graduating seniors who descended in their colorful dresses to receive their diplomas under its spreading branches. In its shade little children played and learned.*
—Broadoaks Kindergarten Normal Training School Brochure 1912

Broadoaks School was founded by two sisters, Ada and Imelda Brooks, who came to California from Iowa in the late 1800s. Both were trained as teachers and were sensitive to the needs of children. In 1906 a mother who knew she had not long to live asked one of the sisters to take her young child and care for him. Other requests followed until the sisters found themselves needing a home for their growing family of five orphaned children. They chose to build their home out of wood on a site filled with oak trees. The two story wood construction was typical of the California bungalow style popular at that time. It was known as the Resident Home for Infants and Young Children. Another house was added on the adjacent property in 1910. This additional space made it possible to expand and include a kindergarten and primary program.

The school, no longer simply a resident home for children, was named Broadoaks and was known as a pioneering venture in early childhood education. It attracted young women interested in learning progressive new teaching methods and teacher training became an added component to the

This huge, arching tree is a remembered image of the school.

Built in 1908 by the Brooks sisters, this home became the Broadoaks School.

A second home was added to the Broadoaks campus in 1910.

children's school. Official recognition of this program at Broadoaks occurred in 1912 when it became a part of the California State Normal Training School program.

The outside environment for the children was always of primary importance to the educational program. More than an acre of land filled with coast live oaks was the setting where children learned. This understanding of the integral relationship between an educational program and its outdoor area is recognized in the school's name, "Broadoaks Outdoor School."

The Trunk:
1920s and 1930s

The location of the school is ideal. The pleasant climate . . . makes it possible to carry on practically all of the work under the great oaks or out in the sunshine. . . . On warm days children sit under the trees, only dampness takes them indoors. Birds and flowers are all about them. . . . A center of interest is an observation hive of bees where queen, worker and drone are distinguished and studied.

—Broadoaks—An Outdoor Kindergarten and Elementary School
1920 School Brochure

Early writings that describe the Broadoaks school create images of place connected to natural elements. Philosophically, it was believed that academic lessons—reading, writing, spelling, and numbers—begin with outdoor activities. The Brooks sisters felt that children's progress was easier "when combined with lessons from nature's wonderful pages" (Brooks 1921, p. 6). Broadoaks welcomed initiative and inventiveness. Discipline was not seen as a problem because the children were so interested in their activities in the out-of-doors. The principal of the Pasadena High School described how the small classes were taught primarily outside with freedom from the restraints of ordinary classrooms, in the abundance of "Nature's own laboratory," and that this environment produced for his son "an almost religious enthusiasm for school" (Brooks 1921, p. 10).

Children take time to eat lunch; their newly built hideout is in the background.

As the teacher training component of the school grew, so did the demands on the existing physical space provided by the two old homes. The boarding program for the very young children and the primary grades were given up as Broadoaks focused on the kindergarten and adult training programs. It was decided to establish Broadoaks as a research laboratory and nursery school. The founders, Ada and Imelda Brooks, continued to experiment with progressive education methods, frequently bringing noted educators to the West Coast to give lectures at Broadoaks.

> *A music lesson is carried out in the tree which shades their tables. . . .*
> *By means of a ladder built for them the bolder ones climb to the*
> *branches, the more timid remaining on the ladder . . . listening to the*
> *bird calls.*
> —Broadoaks—An Outdoor Kindergarten and Elementary School
> 1920 School Brochure

During the late 1920s the Brooks sisters were looking toward retirement and sought a way to assure continuation of their school. Faculty at Whittier College had been involved at Broadoaks as training teachers, and therefore an affiliation with the college already existed. Whittier College was approached as the possible recipient of the sisters' legacy. This was accomplished in 1931 when the school was deeded to the college and became known as Broadoaks School of Education, Whittier College.

The outside physical environment had not changed since the sisters originally housed their orphaned children and began their school in 1908. The large trees remained a major element in the definition of outside spaces for both children and adults. Some play equipment was provided, however, the outside space was primarily used as a place to invent and to discover. Natural materials, such as leaves, flowers, sand, and water, and spare parts, such as boxes and boards, were the primary "play structures."

> *We have constructive materials out of which they build houses large*
> *enough to play in and furniture for their houses.*
>
> *. . . several passenger carrying airplanes were constructed from*
> *materials found on Broadoaks' play grounds and gave entire*
> *satisfaction to their inventors . . . though not one of them ever left the*
> *earth.*
>
> *. . . A beautiful heliotrope dye was discovered by the children in*
> *crushed poppy petals and white cloth was colored by it.*
> Broadoaks—An Outdoor Kindergarten and Elementary School
> 1920 School Brochure

Direct experience with children and their process of learning through play was a key component of the curriculum offered by the School of Education at Whittier College. These experiences took place at Broadoaks. The training program was well known because of its innovative approaches which included use of the out-of-doors as a classroom. It was a flexible environment where children and teachers invented and explored together. During World War II, however, gas rationing and limited resources caused problems in maintaining a lab school on such a distant campus. By 1945 the college trustees authorized the sale of the original Broadoaks school to a group of Pasadena Quakers. The sale included not only the buildings and grounds but also the school's supplies, such as wheel toys, tables, chairs, and so forth.

Pacific Oaks Children's School

The Branches: 1940s and 1950s

The Pacific Oaks Nursery School was founded to realize the Quaker ideals of simplicity, integrity, harmony, and equality. Education for parents and for the adults in the community . . . concerned with the welfare of children and their families offers opportunities for expressing faith in the profound importance and potentiality of every person.
—Pacific Oaks Catalog, 1952

A group of Quaker families purchased Broadoaks School and founded Pacific Oaks Children's School.

Pacific Oaks Friends School was founded when seven families purchased the Broadoaks property from Whittier College in 1945. These families were friends of long-standing and members of the Orange Grove Monthly Meeting of the Religious Society of Friends. They were pacifists who during World War II wished to raise their children in an atmosphere of peace. With their purchase of the Broadoaks property, they set in motion a long-dreamed-of plan of education "from cradle to grave."

Because a nursery school was already functioning on the property, and one of the founding Quaker family members was trained in education, she and her husband accepted the responsibility for living in the original homes and for the general operation of a school. Pacific Oaks Friends School opened with 60 preschool children in 1945.

> *Ample indoor and outdoor space which provide for freedom of movement of all the children is one of our basic assets. Trees, grass, garden space and "digging holes" adjoin the hard surfaces so necessary for wheel-toy activity. The property is extensive enough so that the child who wishes or needs to be by himself can always find a quiet spot to which he can withdraw, until he is ready to rejoin the group. . . . During good weather, most of our time is spend out-of-doors.*
> —Pacific Oaks Bulletin, 1949

The huge oak trees provided a powerful image for the people who developed the children's programs in these early years. The old redwood homes built 50 years ago continued to serve children and adults as an educational setting. The outside spaces dominated by dirt, sand, and plant material continued to be the primary environment where children learned through playful exploration. Teachers worked in the outdoors, creating activities for their young people.

As the founding families began to build their dream on this campus of "cradle to grave education," various adult programs were housed in the buildings formerly used for Broadoaks teacher training classes. A Civilian Public Service Hostel operated on the property for the first five months of 1945 and was succeeded by a Resident Counseling Center. The upstairs interior space was then used for the next four and a half years as an experimental work-study junior college program for young men, sponsored by the Telluride Association of Cornell University. As more adults came to be a part of the educational experience of the nursery school, workshops were given; these led in 1951 to a two-year sequence to train early childhood educators.

Ducks and rabbits live in the southern part of the campus in the Kindergarten Yard.

When a kindergarten program was added in 1950 and located in the South Yard, various cages and shelters for animals were built. Chickens, a bunny, guinea pigs, and a lizard, along with shells, rocks, acorns, flowers, and leaves are described as the teaching materials at Pacific Oaks (school notes, 1949). The importance of creating settings in the out-of-doors to support children's play remained unchanged from the early days of Broadoaks when the Brooks sisters built their dream.

Children using shovels, pulling wagons hitched to trikes, making "cement" from sand, water and mud, moving rocks, tugging planks, barrels, and boxes for bridges or hideouts . . . finding a bug while digging, watching the ducks splashing, this is a very social place!
—Betty James, Parents Bulletin, May 1953

Follow the trail from the front door to the mighty oak between Middle Group and Kindergarten . . . there is a stairway that stretches to the stars.
—Shirley Fields, Parents Bulletin, April 1956

The Foliage: 1960s and 1970s   The adult college programs continued to increase in enrollment, and the physical campus grew with the purchase of an adjacent property on the southwestern edge. The addition of this turn-of-the-century redwood home increased the size of the Pacific Oaks campus and changed the organization of outside physical space for both children and adults.

This increase in acreage of a school located in a single-family residential neighborhood resulted in the city's requiring more off-street parking. The old tennis courts that had been used by children for wheel toys were converted into parking space. However, the greater acreage also made possible the development of a trike area along a small existing pathway located on the western boundary of the property. Used by adults and children, this route developed as a shared wheel toy area. Named Shady Lane, it became the primary circulation path, leading adults beneath the arching trees to the entrances of the various programs for children.

> *The site is organized along a central spine from the parking lot and north entry to the south entry—this is known as Shady Lane and was indeed a former public-access lane. . . . As a child, parent, or visitor enters the site, they move along Shady Lane to the play yards.*
> —Cohen, McGinty and Moore, 1978, p. 329

Plans were needed to remodel the newly acquired home, named Burgess House, for the first president of Pacific Oaks, Evangeline Burgess. Pacific Oaks looked inward to its community of families and staff for talent and expertise to undertake this major design project. Frank Sata, an architect, whose son attended the kindergarten program, was hired to plan the remodeling and then to continue working with the community to develop a master

Shady Lane developed as a wheel toy area and primary circulation path for the community.

plan for the campus. The downstairs spaces were transformed to house a library for adults and children, and upstairs spaces were configured for college research offices. To create quiet, contemplative outside areas adjacent to the interior library rooms, the existing front porch was extended to encircle a large tree. Here, college students could quietly read in a natural and peaceful setting. On the north side of the house, adjacent to the children's library, an outside area was also developed as a special yard for young children. Around an olive tree were built the decks and hull of a small, carefully crafted wooden boat. The textures and beauty of rocks, leaves, light, shadow, and wood enriched this child scaled place. Here children were able to look at books or listen to stories. Both yards were designed to be quiet spaces that took advantage of the natural beauty of the existing trees.

A small boat is built around a tree in the children's yard adjacent to their library.
(Photo by Frank Sata.)

Shady Lane has changed; curving westward in a wider sweep it leads to the Burgess Building. There on the ground floor the library has a beautiful new home with a reading deck for adults. . . . the Children's Patio at the back of the library will have a boat erected in memory of Mary's son . . . patterned after one he designed and built. . . . Frank, father of one of our kindergartners, designed and is overseeing the work. . . . In every feature . . . he has preserved the original Pacific Oaks quality.

—Parents Bulletin, October 1968

Other physical changes that occurred outside during this time include the general maintenance of fences, the rebuilding of sand areas, and the addition of two large play structures. A spool structure known as "Habitat" was added to the south yard, and a molehill with tunneling pipes and raised platform with a cargo net was added as the central feature of "Adventure Yard" (kindergarten primary area). Platforms in tree branches were scattered throughout the outside areas. The design of these structures was generated by the architects working with the Pacific Oaks community.

Using the molehill, above ground or below, is part of the play activity added in the 1960s.

A carpenter hired in 1961 for a few days of carpentry and general maintenance remained at Pacific Oaks for 12 years, building outside areas with the help of teachers, parents, and children. His work with teachers and children had an impact on the built forms and the continued use of loose parts (boxes, boards, ladders) in each of the yards. He believed in involving the children with all phases of work in their play yards.

> *Little kids were all over the place. There were a few of the standard*
> *playthings but not much . . . and there was empty space under the live*
> *oak trees. So I began piling up boxes, boards and ladders for the kids*
> *to climb around on. They loved it. The school insisted I stay on. . . .*
> *The children have always pounded nails and sawed wood right along*
> *with me, helping me make their playthings.*
> —Dawson, in Hillinger 1973

Rapid growth and expansion occurred in the 1970s. In just five years, enrollment doubled in the children's school, now including programs through third grade. Expansion brought with it a strain on and deterioration in physical facilities, caused by crowding and heavy use. The result was a search for additional physical space leading to the consideration of various alternatives. First, Pacific Oaks might purchase and remodel more homes adjacent to the campus, just as property had been acquired in the 1960s.

Perching on boxes, children direct trike traffic in the enlarged turn-around area.

Expansion was opposed by neighbors and therefore rejected by the city. Second, the entire school could relocate on other property. This plan was partially implemented when acreage was purchased in the foothills of northern Pasadena. However, master plans to develop the land and move the campus were never approved by the Pacific Oaks community. There was great hesitancy to relocate, to leave the place that had housed young children since 1906. The entire community felt a deep attachment to this original site, the place where Pacific Oaks first began. Finally, a compromise plan of partial relocation of facilities on a nearby site was approved, and in March 1976 two old homes a mile north were purchased and renovation began. Two years later the college programs moved to the new campus, while the children's programs remained on the original Broadoaks property.

> *These handsome old structures, together with their ample yards and gardens, preserve and embody the ambiance and values of Pacific Oaks. . . . Restoration of the old campus which will remain the site of the Children's School is a part of the expansion. . . . The [original] buildings show the unremitting and increasing use over the years.*
> —The Pacific Oaks New Era, 1977

With the move of adult college programs to a second campus, Pacific Oaks became physically divided and changed. The northern campus developed as the "adult" environment; the original site continued to grow in the types of programs available for children and youth. The college library relocated on the new campus, and Burgess House was converted into a day-care center. As part of this program, two-year-olds moved into the space that had been the children's library. These little ones used the small adjacent Boat Yard, originally intended for quiet stories and reading activities. More sand was added, and various play activities were created with boards, boxes, and other loose parts. A shed built to store these materials became a quiet retreat place, a play house, when not used for spare parts storage.

College research offices moved out of the upper floors of La Loma House, the original Broadoaks Resident Home for Infants and Children. This move provided an opportunity to offer the upstairs space to an alternative high school founded in the early 1970s by Pacific Oaks faculty and directed by Winnie Dorn. Under the director's wise and gentle guidance the program, named the Mini School, was already known in Pasadena as a special nurturing place for teens. During the next eight years these exuberant young folks added a special mix to the comings and goings on the Children's School campus. Some teens worked in the yards with the young children, years later describing how this experience influenced later career decisions.

As the programs continued to expand, the heavily used outside environment was showing signs of wear. Reacting to the increasing physical degradation of the original site, the trustees of Pacific Oaks hired a design team to develop a master plan for the children's school outside spaces. The team from the Art Center College of Design opened an office on the Children's School campus and began observing children and discussing issues with faculty and staff. This interaction between an unfamiliar design team and the Pacific Oaks community generated new thinking about the outdoor space. Teachers used the planning process to carefully analyze their program goals, current use patterns, and problems in their yards. Some of the designers' work was accepted and built, some was rejected or transformed by the teachers ideas. For example, a complete modification of Shady Lane was proposed that would have altered its linear shape and created a large circular community area in its place. Strong opposition was voiced by all sectors of the community. Teachers agreed with the need for community space but came up with their own ideas about its design and location. The proposed master plan served as a catalyst to stimulate teacher's thinking, helping them to clarify issues and make decisions about what they valued.

1980–1985

During the early 1980s, the teachers were searching for direction, ways to think through problems clarified by the recent master planning process. They turned to the past to understand teachers' early use of the yards. The faculty met to review slides of the outside environment taken during the 1950s and 1960s. They wanted to pull together new ideas based on these images of past use. There was a general feeling that many important outside elements shown in the photos were currently missing; perhaps the school's original vision had been changed. It was time to use these past images of outside space use to better understand current and future program goals. They discovered that a focus on permanent play structures was limiting their current thinking.

What supports children creating their own outside environments? Yards used to be 90% flexible; we need more spare parts, we need more private places like in the past; where are our jumping boards, wheelbarrows, wagons, pulleys, turnbuckles? How much of our current environment is manufactured and how much natural as it used to be? We've lost too many old trees. We must protect them and do more planting. Where are our pathways now, why and how do children and adults use them?
—Children's School Faculty Meeting Notes, October 1981

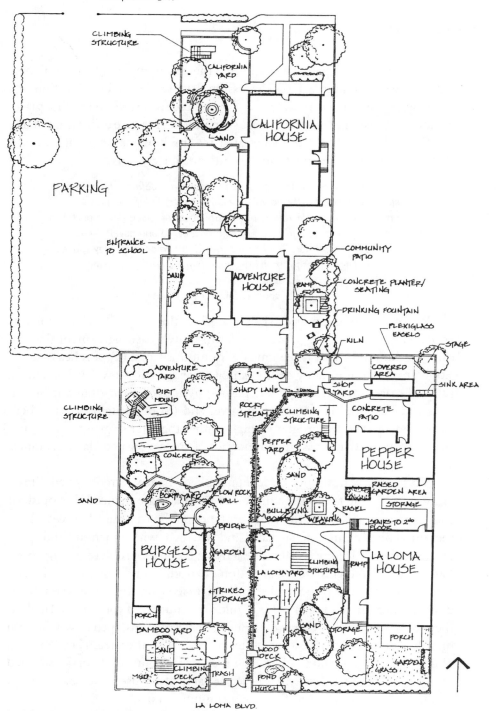

CALIFORNIA BLVD.

CLIMBING STRUCTURE

CALIFORNIA YARD

CALIFORNIA HOUSE

SAND

PARKING

ENTRANCE TO SCHOOL

COMMUNITY PATIO

ADVENTURE HOUSE

SAND

RAMP

CONCRETE PLANTER/ SEATING

DRINKING FOUNTAIN

PLEXIGLASS EASELS

STAGE

KILN

COVERED AREA

SINK AREA

ADVENTURE YARD

DIRT MOUND

SHADY LANE

SHOP YARD

CONCRETE PATIO

CLIMBING STRUCTURE

ROCKY STREAM

CLIMBING STRUCTURE

PEPPER YARD

PEPPER HOUSE

CONCRETE

SAND

RAISED GARDEN AREA

SAND

BOAT YARD

LOW ROCK WALL

BUILDING BOARD

EASEL

STORAGE

WEAVING

STAIRS TO 2ND FLOOR

BRIDGE

BURGESS HOUSE

GARDEN

CLIMBING STRUCTURE

LA LOMA YARD

RAMP

LA LOMA HOUSE

TRIKES STORAGE

PORCH

BAMBOO YARD

SAND

WOOD DECK

SAND

STORAGE

PORCH

GARDEN

GRASS

MUD

CLIMBING DECK

TRASH

POND

HUTCH

LA LOMA BLVD.

Pacific Oaks Children's School Yards.
Play areas, pathways, and community areas after renovation and upgrading of outside spaces in the early 1980s.

Boundaries and pathways between the different programs and their yards were continuing items of discussion. Faculty debated the location of a pathway, a gate, a fence, or the necessity of these structures in the first place. Boundary decisions, figuring out the shape and form these edges might take, whether a barrier could be penetrated by children, or by adults, caused teachers to rethink the entire fabric of the outside campus.

> Boundaries in general serve various purposes: to define—help map space; to protect—the very young child; to clarify—for adult observers; to provide variety and flexible uses of space (loose parts); to soften—plants; to add seclusion and privacy; to add novelty—a multi-sensory barrier. Build boundaries that can become play spaces, by including frames for mobiles, sound (wind chimes), weaving, painting easels and gardens.
> —Children's School Faculty Meeting Notes, November 1981

Renovation of the outside spaces began in the early 1980s and took five years. The changes were part of the community's basic agreement that the campus should provide three kinds of outdoor spaces: (1) porches or transition areas to use in rainy or hot, smoggy weather for low-level activities, (2) yard spaces for various types of play—physical, creative, dramatic, social, constructive, imaginative, and cognitive, and (3) community areas where participants in various programs might gather together in groups and experience activities that cross the boundaries of age-segregated classes (Francis 1990, p. 253).

To create a community space, upper Shady Lane was redesigned. Flowering trees, picnic tables for adults, and resurfacing enhanced this outdoor gathering area located in the main entrance to the campus. The wheel toy section of Shady Lane was surfaced and widened, with a turn-around space created to better accommodate trike activity. Drainage problems along Shady Lane were solved with the construction of an adjacent dry stream bed made from local arroyo stones. Small stone bridges led over this often water-filled drainage area into La Loma Yards. Children, adults, and youth mixed daily as they walked along Shady Lane to their different programs, sped down the path on trikes, or paused to investigate water moving along the stream bed. Parents, children, teenagers, and teachers ate lunch in the community patio, stopped a moment there to chat with someone, and often used the space to sell T-shirts, food, or tickets to future community events.

Deteriorating wood play structures in the yards were removed, and other structures, with flexible parts, were added. Sand areas were enlarged and rebuilt away from the root systems of the native oak trees. Shrubbery,

The community patio is a gathering place for parents, teachers, and children.

flowers, and raised vegetable gardens were reintroduced, elements that had existed in the school's past. A lawn was planted in the south part of the campus in front of the original Brooks sisters home. This small contrasting soft green space was nurtured by the preschool faculty member who taught there, feeling that it would add a needed dimension to her program. After she retired 10 years later, the grass did not survive.

Each Children's School building was evaluated in terms of transitional spaces, places where the outside yard met the inside classroom. Porches on La Loma House were expanded to accommodate tables for quiet activities. The upstairs porch was also enlarged, making it possible for the teenagers to observe the young children playing below. A porch was added to the north side of Burgess House for the youngest day-care children. The small building originally known in the 1940s as "termite hall" was remodeled, and an outdoor patio was included in this renovation.

A stream bed along Shady Lane invites exploration.

The entrance to campus was softened with planting. Fences were rebuilt, and pathways/boundaries redesigned to include adult seating. The major edge between two programs was clarified by a variety of structures that would facilitate different play activities. This "activity fence" included a linking of a various forms: a Plexiglas easel, a bench seating platform around an oak tree, large smooth stones, a raised bed garden, a frame for weaving, and a wooden bar on which to hang child-created mobiles. Although the structures built to support these activities were permanent, the color, texture, and look of the boundary changed as children planted flowers, wove with colorful strands, painted on the Plexiglas, and hung their wind chimes and mobiles.

**The Whole-
Design Process**

As a 90-year-old setting for children, the outside environment of Pacific Oaks has remained remarkably the same. Large trees tower above the yards, shading old redwood-frame turn-of-the-century homes. Sand and dirt dominate the surfaces where children make magic potions and wagons hitched to trikes traverse Shady Lane. Growth and expansion have created environmental problems of dust, degeneration of plant material, and erosion, but the basic philosophical belief in the importance of the outside environment as a place where children have the greatest opportunity to imagine, to create and to dream, and, ultimately, to learn, is still the core of this school.

During the late 1970s a project entitled Environments for Play and Child Care conducted by a team drawn from the Community Design Center at the University of Wisconsin-Milwaukee Center for Architecture and Urban Planing Research studied Pacific Oaks as one of their sites. The team compiled data through on-site observations and user interviews. The purpose of the project was to generate a design guide and technical manual for a department of the Army that was planning new day-care facilities and play areas. A key word in their description of the design process is evolved.

> The process of design at Pacific Oaks is interesting. No master plan has been adopted, no architects retained. . . . The early history of the School evolved around former houses, their backyards, and a communal lane. All additions and changes have been evolutionary and incremental. All work has been done by parents and staff, all design likewise. . . . the School feels fortunate to count two architects among its parents, and they have assisted in design and construction of equipment.
>
> —Pacific Oaks Archives 1978

Although an outside design team was hired in 1979, the evolutionary process described by the University of Wisconsin draft report continues to apply. The physical changes that occurred in the outside environment during the 1980s were generated by teachers, often in response to designers' suggestions.

The school continues to hire from among past and present parents; architects, landscape architects, contractors, and carpenters who were currently, or had been, a part of the Pacific Oaks community. Families still help with building and upgrading the outside spaces, although fewer are able to actively donate their time because of economic or child care pressures. Teachers continue to be in charge of the spaces they use. Now, nearly a hundred years later, the outside environment of this school still reflects the original vision of Ada and Imelda Brooks and the continuing goals of the seven Quaker families—an outdoor educational environment where children can experience the joy of discovery, test their ideas in action, and observe the results with a sense of wonder.

HIGH SCHOOL ENVIRONMENT CASE STUDY
Midland School, Los Olivos, California

**The Roots:
1930s**

Driving along a two lane back road, wandering through the oak-studded grassy hills of the central coast of California, one encounters the unexpected sign,"Midland," its simple letters carved in wood, set in a base of local rocks. The Midland school is grounded in the vision of its founder, Paul Squibb , who wanted to build a "simple life" school for boys. The founder's primary goal was to create an educational environment that minimized buildings, equipment, and services in favor of careful study, an outdoor life, and

Ranch property selected by the Squibbs as the ideal location for a high school.

self-help. Midland was born during the depression years, and it fit philosophically with the necessities of those difficult times.

The school's location was an important, major first task. The Squibbs
wanted a site to take advantage of the cooling effect of the Pacific Ocean but
away from the coast and equally distant from San Francisco and Los Angeles.
Their choice was thus limited to a narrow strip of land between Santa Barbara
and San Luis Obispo, known then as Midland Counties.

In 1932, the Los Librillos lease of a 5,000 acre section of La Laguna Ranch
was being vacated by default. The Squibbs took over the remainder of the
grazing lease and bought "three of the horses, a wagon, some tools and
furniture with an old mare and a lot of worn-out machinery thrown in." By
1941 the school was able to purchase a portion of its leased land, a total school
ownership of 2,860 acres, which is the current land holding and boundary
of Midland School.

From its original 1845 Mexican grant days the property was largely
undeveloped and seldom inhabited except for grazing. From 1908 until
Midland School began, a succession of tenants leased the land and had
various partnership arrangements with the owners, La Laguna Ranch Corporation. Most of the original school buildings were built immediately after
World War I, before the collapse of farm prices in the late 1920s. When
Midland School opened in 1932, the structures included the horse barn, the
main house, and some sheds and storerooms.

*Large native oaks surround
the original ranch home built
in the early 1900s.*

It was pretty bare as far as the ground looked. There was no growth much except for the handsome big native trees. And it was also covered with baling wire and tin cans, mostly tobacco cans, and turkey feathers and old farm machinery parked every place . . . it was beautiful.

—Papers in Midland archives, Benedict Rich 1932

Paul Squibb described this home for Midland School as a place where a boarding school could be a utility rather than a luxury. He also believed this meaning would be evident in the school's physical form. He believed that people needed to learn that "money, food, light, heat and water are not things that flow naturally out of pipes but things for which someone has to spend time, thought and energy." There was no heat in the living quarters during those early years. Students chopped wood to build fires to heat water for showers and to heat the classrooms, which had small wood burning stoves. There was no electric power. Students used small oil lamps to study by in the evenings. All of the maintenance, repair, and construction work was completed from within the Midland community. Seldom were people hired from the outside to help with design, construction, remodeling, or maintenance.

The school opened in 1932 with its first class of nine teenage boys and four teachers. A large metal triangle was rung to call together the first school assembly in the downstairs of the Main House. Sixty years later the sound still rings out from the porch of the dining hall, calling students to assembly.

The triangle hanging on the edge of the dining hall porch is still rung at meal times.

The school doubled in size the second year, and by 1939 it enrolled 61 students, considered the best size for a school of this type at the time. The seventh and eighth grades formed a lower school, ninth and tenth grades a middle school, and eleventh and twelfth grades an upper school. Mr. Squibb, with his wife, lived in the main farmhouse for 18 years, running Midland as its founding headmaster.

In the beginning the boys built their own living quarters, called "shacks," out of simple board-and-batten construction. If the students wanted to improve their living area, the school would provide the materials after the boys submitted plans for their project. The classrooms were also built out of wood with double joists and rafters at 10-foot intervals to allow for cutting and moving, if necessary, during the time the land was leased rather than owned. Desks designed in the 1930s by a faculty member, and built by the students, are still being used today. Faculty and students cooked, served, and ate meals together, first in the Main House and by 1934 in Stillman Hall, which serves as a gathering area for assemblies and a study hall in the evenings.

The original horse barn has always been a strong landmark at Midland. It is one of the first structures a visitor sees, driving on the dirt road across Alamo Pintado river. The barn has been the setting for a variety of physical activities in addition to the horse program. During the early years it was the location of intramural wrestling . It also provided various ways to create physically challenging activities; the boys set up a conveyer track at the ridge

Called "shacks," the original living areas for teens (males) had no heat.

The horse barn is a strong landmark on the Midland campus.

pole of the barn for swinging. A tradition of throwing students in the horse trough on their birthdays was celebrated for years at the barn, which has remained a favorite place for students to simply "hang out."

Sycamore trees grow along the river that runs through the school's property, which floods the banks during winter storms and remains dry during the hot summer months. Large native oaks shade the Main House and dominate the north-facing slopes of the adjacent hills. In the distance are views of Grass Mountain and the wilderness areas beyond. A reservoir located in the eastern part of the property is always a popular place for students to relax, play with rafts, swim, swing on ropes hanging from the trees, or just sit and enjoy the beauty of the setting. Camping trips, opportunities to learn from the natural environment surrounding Midland, are an important part of the curriculum and daily life. Horses are used to explore the adjacent hills, Grass Mountain, Indian Mound, and the back country.

> *It was a great pleasure to have that flowing water in the spring . . . it was play rather than work. . . . The reservoir provided a somewhat muddy pond in which reed rushes and cattails grew . . . we enjoyed a place to play with rafts, boats, and to swim. We had a sort of diving board including ropes hanging from trees [from] which one could swing or go flying out and land with a splash in the middle of the reservoir.*
> —Paul Squibb, Letters 1933–1983

Chicken sheds and a storage room were converted into a small nonsectarian chapel, where the names of all Midland students and faculty are listed

Teens enjoy "hanging out" at the school reservoir, a place of retreat for students.

on the walls. These names are listed according to the year a student or faculty began at Midland, regardless of graduation. The belief is that if a person spent only one year at Midland he or she is a part of the school community and should be recognized as such.

A small storage structure initially used to repair farm machinery was later named the "car barn" when it became the maintenance and storage shed for the school's 1932 Ford station wagon. This area is an outside classroom where everyone can learn welding, auto mechanics, electrical wiring, and general repair and maintenance. Its yard is a collection of stuff, items that ordinarily might be thrown away in other settings, but here are a symbol of the importance of fixing things. Through the years this area has the accumulation of unfinished projects—spare parts for someone's inventive dream.

A classroom known as Lumber Yard was built as a three-walled shed to store the timber purchased by the school when the Los Olivos railroad station was torn down in 1935. After the lumber was used, the space served as a much needed classroom. As a shed, it is completely open on the east side; however, students still attend daily classes in Lumber Yard, even during cold and wet winter weather.

The buildings of the original ranch, dating back to 1917, and the additional structures that were built on the property in the 1930s to house the school make up the core of the current Midland School campus. In keeping with the school's philosophy and the vision of its founder, it was

A student practices welding outside in the car barn work area.

Built as a place to store lumber, this classroom is open on one side. School desks built in the 1930s are still used.

built by faculty and students with a minimum use of materials or outside input and "making do with things at hand" whenever possible.

> *We want this to be a community where each person is concerned for*
> *each other . . . where we try to make the most of what we have to*
> *work with.*
> —Paul Squibb, Letters 1933–1983.

Unlike many other schools, Midland requires its students to participate in maintaining their environment. Each has a job that is vital to the running of the school, from waiting on tables to plumbing, from chopping wood to provide heat to caring for the school's horses.

> *It is a philosophy of self-sufficiency. Midland has always attempted to*
> *meet its needs from within, there are no maintenance crews,*
> *gardeners, nor hired dishwashers at Midland. No one cleans up after*
> *the students. Everyone living at Midland does the work.*
> —Midland archives, 1980

The Trunk:
1940s

The rationing and unavailability of materials during World War II strengthened the resolve of those who taught and learned at Midland. In a search for any available building materials, some surplus windows and frames were located. By constructing the one room classroom with more windows, less wood siding would be needed—a scarce resource at this time. With windows running the length of all four walls, the building was named the Glass House.

In 1948 electricity was brought to the property line. Paul Squibb felt it would have been "artificial" not to install electric power on campus. Although the experience of living without electricity was valued, electrification lessened the danger of fire created by the oil lamps.

An area known as the Faculty Coffee Tree became a traditional outdoor gathering place for teachers in the early years. Under this black walnut tree, faculty met daily during the morning recess to share a cup of coffee and relax during their break. Meeting here also became an end-of-the-day ritual. The umbrella-shaped tree provided pleasant shade until it died in the 1980s. However, even without the tree, the tradition of teachers' gathering outside each morning in this particular place continues today. The area is still called the Coffee Tree, although only a stump remains.

The Glass House classroom was constructed out of surplus windows during World War II.

Faculty at Midland still gather for morning break around the Coffee Tree, even though only a stump remains.

The Branches: 1950s and 1960s

The Main House, the dining hall, and the chapel formed a strong triangular core of the central Midland campus. Everyone used the three buildings many times during the day. No one could go to class or return to the living areas without passing through this area. The Squibbs lived in the Main House, located in the "heart" of this core; therefore, authority was also central to this

The Main House housed the founding headmaster and his wife until retirement.

area because it housed the headmaster. He was never far from the school's center and thus in touch with the community.

> *The circulation and arrangement was like a complete organization that no one escaped. There was an organic feel, a pulse that went on in and around these three buildings. This pulse involved the entire school. The arrangement of the buildings in this triangle, was a great strength of Midland in the early years.*
> —Midland School Archives, unpublished papers

The Squibbs moved out of the Main House in 1950 as the first step in retirement. Although the Main House has always been the administration hub, the core of the school changed when the Squibbs moved, because no other headmaster has lived in the Main House since.

The library was first housed in the Main House. In the 1950s the Willrich Memorial Building was built as a library. The L-shape of the building encloses an outside space adjacent to the Main House that was paved with stones gathered from the nearby river. Picnic benches located in this outside area are shaded by large native trees. This space is used as an outside classroom or as a quiet retreat and study area.

New cabins, known as Panabodes, were built to replace the original shacks. These two-room log cabins housed four boys, two to a room. Some of the older structures were kept as living areas for incoming

The students' living area, cabins known as Panabodes, have wood-burning stoves for heat.

freshmen. Without heat, the original structures were felt to represent the school's founding value of austerity; they were used into the late 1980s. In contrast, the new Panabodes included small wood-burning stoves and became the upper-classmen's area of the campus.

Although boys continued to build shacks, these structures no longer housed the students and functioned only as get-away retreats. Sometimes the shacks were built in trees or on hillsides, nestled among the brush. These often elaborate structures were private sanctuaries and completely controlled by the boys who built them. Ownership and control of privacy was respected by everyone. The shacks were willed, as legacies, with serious implications and passed down from graduating seniors to the boys in the next class. With the impact of the 1960s' drug problems, allowing students to build and use such private areas became a matter of extreme concern to the faculty and headmaster. Strict consequences, including immediate dismissal for serious rule infractions, were agreed upon, and the building of personal retreat spaces continued well into the 1980s without significant incidents.

**The Foliage:
1970s and 1980s**

The first group of female students was enrolled in 1977. The girls lived upstairs in the Main House in what had been the infirmary and nurse's home. This major change, to a coeducational school, resulted in clearer delineation of boundaries, places where students could and couldn't go on campus during particular times. The eastern part of campus, known as upper yard, developed as the boys' area. The western part of campus, around the Infirmary, developed as the girls' area. Separation of these areas during specific times was strictly enforced. Privacy needs and visiting procedures between males and females in the living areas were clearly defined by both regulations on behavior and geographic space.

Because the infirmary was always considered only a temporary female student living space, Whittier Quad was built in the early 1980s to provide housing more consistent with the boys' two-room two-person cabins. Four cabins surrounding the shower house/bathroom building were built in the meadow west of the infirmary, further emphasizing the division between the male and female living areas of the campus.

**The Whole-
Design Process**

During Midlands' 60 years of operation, the built environment has evolved. Physical changes have happened slowly and have always been completed by the community in a way believed to be consistent with the goals and values of the school. The original horse barn remains a central structure and campus landmark. The walls of a small nonsectarian chapel display the year and names of all Midland students. The original post office/store is still a gathering place for mail pickup. The flag pole in front, a gift of the class of 1937, is a silhouette against the sky. The front porch of the main farmhouse is a popular gathering place. Cabins are heated by wood stoves, and hot showers are available only in the afternoons when those students on "shower duty" build the fires to heat the water. All maintenance is carried out by faculty and students. At graduation an award is given for the student who did the best job of "making do with things at hand."

Although the evolution of built form has happened slowly, there are physical remnants of leftover dreams of both faculty and students. Each graduating class plans a project, something the class will build as their legacy. A class gift of picnic tables outside the library are heavily used today. On the other hand, an amphitheater built into a hillside proved to be beyond the ability, time, energy, and commitment of one senior class. Although the land is scarred, erosion and plants have begun to reclaim this hillside space, once

The flagpole in front of the post office was a class gift to Midland.

the subject of heated decision making among teenagers trying to figure out how to leave a permanent and useful landmark at their school.

Over the years the campus has experienced severe physical deterioration because of growth and expansion, intense use as a school facility, and delayed maintenance. Dust during the hot weather, mud and flooding in the rainy season are indicators of soil erosion caused by traffic, which has resulted in a loss of ground cover and trees. In 1991, for the first time in its history, the Midland community and its board of directors decided to develop a long-range master plan for the land. A former Midland student from the 1950s currently a practicing designer, volunteered to begin this work. Although Midland is still true to its philosophy of self-sufficiency and meeting needs from within, there is also recognition of the importance of a consultant in the process of planning and design.

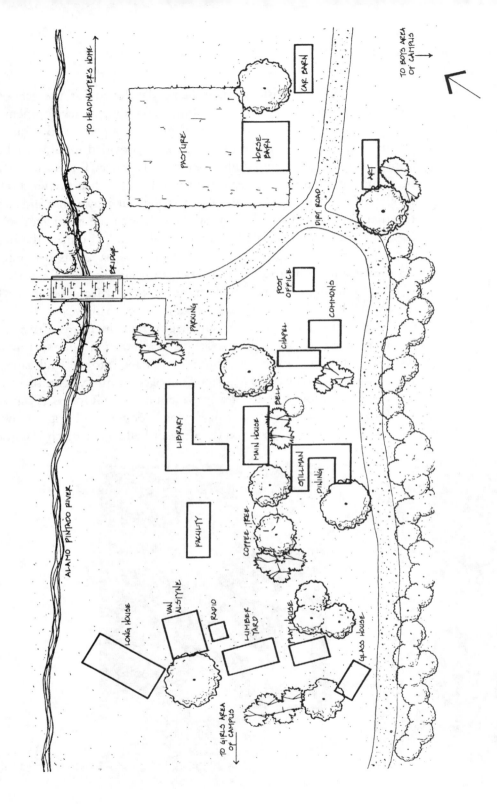

Midland School Core Campus.
Primary buildings and outside environment used by the community.

Even though a master plan is being developed for the school, the community of faculty, students, and alumni is guiding its development. Each change in pathway, proposed structure, addition of plants and seating areas happens only after faculty and students have provided input, raised questions, and voiced concerns. Students expressed the need for a social gathering place and in the early 1990s began working closely with an architect (class of 1959) to plan their special "warm place to hang-out, play games and have fun together" (*Midland Mirror*, 1994). Students helped the contractor (class of 1968) pour the cement slab, build the framing, and complete the dry wall construction. At completion in the fall of 1993, students decorated the northwest wall with pictures of the graduating classes from the early 1970s to the present and named the building after a former faculty member/headmaster and his wife who had lived on campus for many years.

The visions of its founder are still shaping the built forms of this campus. Young people understand their social history in the everyday surroundings, its artifacts that are not set apart but incorporated into the landscape, used, played with, seen daily. The Midland School community continues to pride itself in its traditions that are clearly evident in its built forms. A school bell salvaged in the early days from a nearby one-room school rings out 60 years later; students are still assigned the duty of bell ringer. Each classroom is

The school bell is rung by a Midland student assigned the duty of "bell ringer."

unique, a structure that tells a story in the way it was built and the materials used. Over time, students and faculty have named these forms—Glass House, Lumber Yard, Play House, Janeway, vanAlstyne, Stillman, Pink Elephant, Long House—which represent some of the school's history, as shared community knowledge, create continuity, and provide meaning. The images of this school, its bell that schedules the day, the old desks, the barn, the chapel walls covered with names, a farmhouse front porch, arching oak trees, and wood stoves are imprints on the "landscape of the mind" and, as placemakers impart a strong sense of belonging.

> *The Midland philosophy of thrift and paying your way may seem stuck in the mud; but even in that position, one can keep the matches dry, and light an occasional candle for a world suffering from squandered resources and over population.*
> —Letter from Paul Squibb to Graduates, Class of 1982

Alike/Different— A Summary

The case histories of the two educational environments presented here show striking similarities in five areas of their evolution. First, a guiding vision was nurtured throughout the schools' histories. Second, the design process evolved from within. Third, the original built forms are consciously preserved. Fourth, maintenance and building physical structures are part of the schools' curriculum. Fifth, the outside space is used as a classroom. Valuing the natural environment has been a defining physical aspect of each campus for children, youth, and adults alike.

Each school was founded by people with a very clear vision based on their value system, which they applied to educational pedagogy. The physical form of the property they purchased was seen as having the potential to support that vision, and the values in both schools emphasized simplicity rather than consumption. Judging what is needed, rather than what is wanted, results in using resources carefully and changing in small increments over time. This is an evolutionary process over an extended period, allowing teachers to be involved in place making rather than limited to maintaining what others design and build. It allows designers to work within a community, understanding its past and creating its future as a something that will have meaning because it evolves from the group most directly affected by its eventual form.

In both settings adults were able to design, arrange, and change their settings. At Midland, faculty actually built their own homes on the school land and at Pacific Oaks teachers created "habitats," mud holes, and activity fences. Both environments at any given point were more likely to be "in process" than complete. Both settings provided physical space for the adults and youth to try out ideas, see whether they work, change the physical environment, and learn from the results. Problems arose in both settings when a teacher who created a particular kind of environment was no longer there, using that space. The car barn at Midland is filled with mechanical dreams, never completed, taking up space, a legacy to some teachers' favorite project with students. The hillside is scarred with the beginnings of an amphitheater students planned but which ended with their graduation. An educational setting that supports process will have problems with what to do with its leftover environments.

The built forms at both settings are simple wood construction, not difficult to build or to change. However, both environments changed their old structures very little. Most of the original buildings remain on the sites as reminders of what came before and a statement of how future physical structures should look. Over time these built forms have become the school's defining landmarks.

In the schools' philosophy maintenance is viewed as a part of what is learned; everyone participates, adults and young people alike. At Pacific Oaks, children watched and helped Russell repair fences as often as they used swings and trikes. At Midland everyone has a job, from the early years of "head lampman" to "electrician" after electric power was added. Because young people are allowed to help build and to maintain their physical environment, they feel an integral part of the school. On the other hand, there is just so much maintenance that can be done from within. The emphasis on simplicity, process and the use of wood has added to the deterioration of buildings on both campuses. This problem becomes more severe when maintenance is delayed owing to lack of funds or because of the philosophical emphasis on simplicity and thrift.

The natural environment is a powerful force in the outside areas of both schools. Education happens among the trees as much, if not more, than within walls. The outside offers students opportunities to explore and manipulate their environment. They are able to "mess around" outside, building shacks in the trees or digging pools in the mud.

Teachers value the opportunity to teach about what is close at hand; trees, insects, streams, and critters are all part of the curriculum. Special areas are set aside so that the people who work and learn in that setting are always in proximity to animal life. The Midland pig wandered the campus in the early years as a needed garbage disposal, helping to solve food waste problems. A blind raccoon, a pet during the 1940s, amazed students when he caught, washed, and ate goldfish from the horse trough. The Pacific Oaks ducks provided eggs for morning pancake-making activities. Art happens in both settings outside, under the trees. The structures built to house art activities are minimal, a place to sit where the light and shadow of eucalyptus leaves are captured and enjoyed in the early morning breeze.

The concern about the degradation of the natural environment, the loss of oak trees, the erosion of soils, the possibility that the ecology of the outside space was not being respected is evident at both schools. This was one motivation to seek help and to begin a careful process of planning and design that better understands and protects the natural systems on each site. At Midland students live close to the beauty and dangers in their natural environment. In 1993 a devastating fire burned within two miles of the school's central two-acre core and damaged hundreds of acres of surrounding land. The river running through the school's property has flooded its banks during severe winter storms. Studying the recovery of this landscape from natural disasters and understanding ecological systems is an increasingly important part of the high school curriculum.

There has always been a clarity of purpose in both settings, established by the founders and nourished by those who followed. The sites were chosen by the people who planned to run the programs. The environment as a "particular place" was recognized as supporting the original vision. Physical changes to either campus are evaluated against the goals of the school, and this process helps to clarify what should or shouldn't be done. Decisions are

Midland students and faculty work on sculpture in an outside art studio.

Art is produced outside, under the trees, at the Pacific Oaks Art Studio.

Feeding the ducks and gathering their eggs are part of the daily routine at school.

never far removed from the basic value system of the people who will feel their impact. Neither of the schools is an "all-purpose" setting but each takes a particular point of view and has the luxury of providing a defined educational choice for teachers and children. This clear value orientation is unlike that of many educational settings where decisions seem to be made by rule books, efficiency, and cost.

Both schools exhibit an evolution of forms that invite problem solving by the players. Here, the freedom and challenge to manipulate the environment according to community needs is a design process over time. Although neither setting is without major environmental problems, the history of these "particular places" helps us understand a process of creating educational settings that support young people, teachers, and designers working together as problem solvers.

References

Chawla, Louise. 1992. "Childhood place attachments." In *Place Attachment,* edited by I. Altman and S. Low. New York: Plenum Press.

Children's School Faculty Meeting Notes, 1980-1985, Pacific Oaks College and Children's School, Pasadena, CA.

Cooper Marcus, Clare. 1992. "Environmental memories." In *Place Attachment,* edited by I. Altman and S. Low. New York: Plenum Press.

Downing, Frances. 1992. "The role of place and event imagery in the act of design." *The Journal of Architectural and Planning Research* 9:(1): 64–77.

Flemming R., and R. Von Tscharner. 1981. *Place Makers.* New York: Hastings House.

Francis, Carolyn. 1990. "Day care outdoor spaces." In *People Places: Design Guidelines for Urban Open Space,* edited by C. Cooper Marcus and C. Francis. New York: Van Nostrand Reinhold.

Hart, Roger. 1979. *Children's Experience of Place.* New York: Irvington Press.

Hester, Randy T. 1985. "Subconscious landscapes of the heart." *Places* 2(3): 10–22.

Hillinger, A. 1973. "Carpenter becomes expert in teaching preschool children." *Times* 17 April, Part II.

Pacific Oaks Archives Draft Report, "Environment for play and childcare project" Cohen, McGinty, and Moore, 1978, Pasadena, CA.

Moore, Robin. 1990. *Childhood's Domain: Play and Place in Child Development.* Berkeley, CA: MIG Communications.

The Pacific Oaks New Era 1976-78. Annual Report, Pacific Oaks College and Children's School. Pasadena, CA: Pacific Oaks College.

Parents' Bulletins Pacific Oaks Nursery School, 1949-1970. Pasadena, CA.

Proshansky, Harold and Abbe Fabian. 1987. "The development of place identity in the child." In *Spaces for Children: The Built Environment and Child Development*, edited by C. Weinstein and T. David. New York: Plenum Press.

Rossi, Aldo. 1981. *A Scientific Autobiography.* Cambridge, MA: MIT Press.

Squibb, Paul. "History of Midland School" unpublished papers, 1957, Los Olivos, CA (Midland Archives).

Walter, Eugene V. 1988. *Placeways.* NC: University of North Carolina, Chapel Hill.

Wilgress, Jane, ed. 1992. *"Yours Somewhat truly . . . Selections from the Letters of Paul Squibb 1933–1983.* Los Olivos, CA: Midland School.

Wolfe, Maxine and Leanne Rivlin. 1987. "The institutions in children's lives." In *Spaces for Children: The Built Environment and Child Development*, edited by C. Weinstein and T. David. New York: Plenum Press.

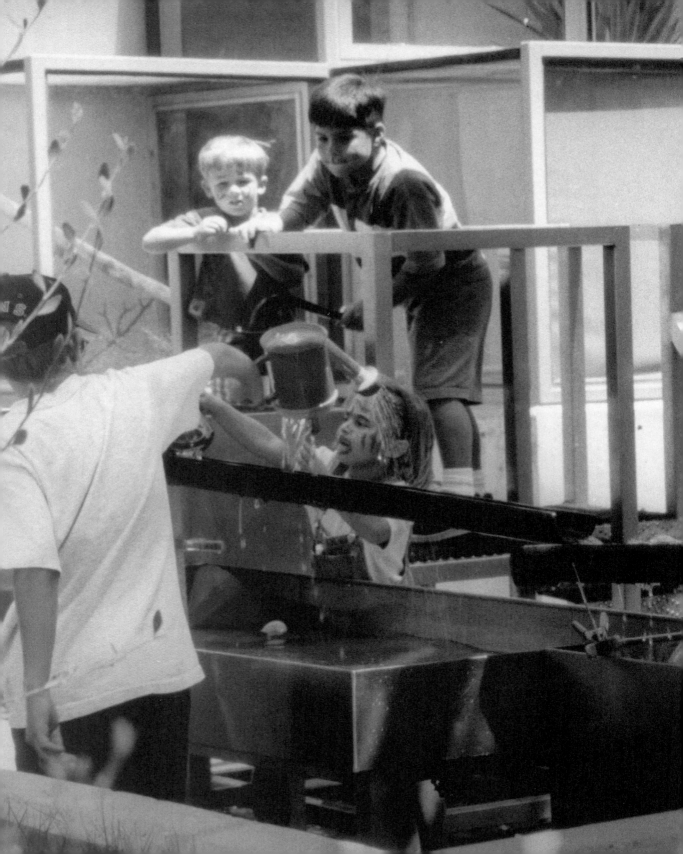

4

CONGRUENCE

INTRODUCTION

The environment is an active and pervasive influence on the lives of children and teachers throughout the school day. It provides the setting for learning and at the same time acts as a participant in teaching and learning. In thinking about introducing this chapter, my friend and colleague Joseph Suina's experiences first came to mind. I then realized the introduction was already written: his childhood memories vividly describe his feelings about the importance of fit between people and place.

"Grandmother and I lived beside the plaza in a one-room house. Inside, we had a traditional fireplace, a makeshift cabinet for our few tin cups and bowls, and a wooden crate that held our two buckets of all-purpose water. At the innermost part of the room were two rolls of bedding we used as comfortable sitting couches. Tucked securely beneath my blankets, I listened to her stories, how it was when she was a little girl, her soft singing; in this way, I went off to sleep each night.

"The winter months are among my fondest memories. A warm fire crackled and danced brightly in the fireplace, and the aroma of delicious stew filled our one-room house. The thick adobe walls wrapped around the two of us protectingly during the long freezing nights. To me, the house was just right. Grandmother's affection completed the warmth and security I will always remember.

"Barefooted, I greeted the sun each morning with a handful of cornmeal. At night I'd look to the stars in wonderment and let a prayer slip through my lips. I learned to appreciate cooperation in nature and with my fellow men early in life. I felt very much a part of the world and our way of life. I knew I had a place in it, and I felt good about it. And then I went to school.

"School was a new and bewildering experience . . . the strange surroundings, new ideas, expectations, and foreign tongue were at times overwhelming to us beginners. The classroom had its odd characteristics. It was terribly huge and smelled of medicine like the village clinic I feared so much. The walls and ceiling were artificial and uncaring. They were too far from me and I felt naked. Those fluorescent light tubes made an eerie drone and blinked suspiciously over me. This was quite a contrast to the fire and sunlight my eyes were accustomed to. Our confinement to rows of desks was another unnatural demand made on our active little bodies. Running carefree in the village and fields was but a sweet memory of days gone by."

—CATHERINE LOUGHLIN AND JOSEPH SUINA

Every setting has a program and people who are responsible for this. When the setting and the behavior fit, it can be described as congruent.

—Barker 1968, p. 186

Fit

◆*It is essential that the people do shape their surroundings for themselves.*

—Alexander 1979, p. 354

We push the edges of places to fit ourselves, to meet our needs, to reflect what we value. Effecting a good fit between a physical setting and the people who use it includes challenges and problems similar to those involved in selecting something to wear. In choosing clothing, we are limited by size, resources, need, comfort, and personal preference. The expertise of a fashion designer or skill of a tailor enriches the kinds of choices offered and helps us see new possibilities. Our clothing feels like a part of us when the match is right. We also know when there is a lack of fit, when our clothing does not provide physical comfort—protection from heat, cold, sun, or moisture—or social comfort—to fit the occasion, the culture, or the image. Whether for social or physical reasons, a misfit is uncomfortable. We evaluate the problem and make changes.

We also know immediately upon entering a physical setting whether there is an absence of fit between the environment and the behavior of the people using it. Like clothing, a setting may not provide physical comfort; it may be too hot, cold, or windy or lack sufficient protection from moisture. The environment may feel unsafe. Physical support, such as places to sit or easy ways to move about, may be missing. Social comfort may also be a problem if there are no visible connections between the physical environment and the user's identity, cultural background, or the type of activity that takes place. The problem of lack of fit between a setting and its users, unfortunately, is not as easily remedied as changing inappropriate or uncomfortable clothing. The icy chill of an ocean wind is no longer uncomfortable when a down jacket is added, but an empty, windswept expanse of concrete that feels unsafe, cold, and boring often remains uncomfortable because change involves layers of complexity beyond the simple addition of a piece of clothing.

Fatigue occurs when adults don't know where their space is, when they cannot find the places that fit them comfortably. When designing a "good

91

place," one that fits the children and the adults who use it, there must be flexibility to make changes that support a variety of uses and to accommodate design and development over time. According to Lynch (1981 p. 142), "A good place is one which is, in some way, appropriate to the person and her culture, makes her aware of her community, her past, the web of life, and the universe of time and space in which these are contained."

Educational settings are arranged and rearranged according to cultural values, personal preferences, theoretical understanding, professional goals, and children's needs and behavior. For example, in a large city near Los Angeles, teachers in adjacent schools, an extended day child-care program and a junior high school woodshop class, discussed a piece of unused land on their school districts property. Adults in both settings agreed that it was a waste of valuable outdoor space in that crowded metropolitan area. The vacant corner was filled with weeds and enclosed by a chain link fence. It looked abandoned, a space never used by children, a place that simply accumulated trash tossed over the fence. The teachers began to discuss the problem and possibilities of using this area. They shared a concern that children seldom experience the process and products of gardening. A program for a co-op garden in the unused corner lot was developed. Teachers' goals and values became evident in the physical forms they created. They began to push the edges of that space to fit their needs.

◆*Destyne saw green beans coming from the ground. "They're waking up, our garden is waking up!"*
Joyce Mortara-Shoop, teacher, Willard Children's Center
Documentation of gardening curriculum, March 1993

The teachers sought help from within the community, in particular from people with an expertise in gardening and construction, and a raised bed garden plan evolved. Eight planter boxes were built, painted, and filled with dirt by the junior high school students enrolled in woodshop classes. The young children attending the child-care facility carefully planted vegetables and flowers. A year-round schedule of daily care resulted in new taste treats, critter discoveries, and a developing sense of wonder in the natural cycles of growth and change. Teachers began to realize their goal of providing hands-on discovery and exploration in growing food. Children experienced the results of productive work. A setting once lacking congruence was changed to fit the daily activities of both the child care-program and the junior high school shop curriculum. An abandoned, litter-cluttered vacant lot became "our garden."

Vision

*◆From old photographs . . . we discovered that the school site had
been under cultivation in the 1920s [with] chickens, rabbits, a goat. .
. . Gardening went out of fashion and was replaced by asphalt—most
likely as part of a post-W.W.II neat-and-tidy engineering approach to
school environments.*

—Moore 1995, p. 224

Historically, the primary purpose of outside school areas was to help children
develop physically through sports and games (Adams 1993). Team activity
shaped the field areas adjacent to schools. Playground form was a reflection
of current educational philosophy. For example, the military model, popular
during the first half of the twentieth century, reflects control and contain-
ment. Outside spaces were large expanses of asphalt surrounded by high
chain link fencing and looked like military drill yards. Children were organized into lines and played games with rules. Seating areas were often used
for discipline, i.e., a player was "benched" or removed from the activity for
breaking a rule. Games were seen as a way to "build character" as well as to
help children develop physically. An industrial model, more evident after
the Second World War, took on the appearance of a factory, where produc-
tion and achievement were emphasized (Adams 1993). Outside, children
were expected to release the physical tension built up after sitting inside at
their desks. The belief at the time was that children would be better able to
produce intellectually if provided breaks for physical activity on the playground. As in a factory, with its mandated coffee breaks, children move
between the inside and outside spaces when bells ring on predictable schedules. The design of the environment reflects the ideas, attitudes, and ethics
of the time. The vision of those in charge is often based on the criteria that
equipment is long lasting and maintenance free and that insurance compa-
nies approve. The influence of the military and factory models is still visible
in the physical form of school playgrounds. School grounds look strikingly
similar. They lack the unique stamp of a particular culture. The collective
experience of a community who designs and uses the space is missing in the
visible form.

　　An outside environment can reflect the uniqueness of its location,
activities, and users. Midland High School and Broadoaks/Pacific Oaks
Children's School are examples of built and natural physical forms that
mirror the ongoing vision of the teachers, families, children, and designers
who impact the setting. The location and unique physical features of both
sites and the kinds of activities that take place out-of-doors describe a vision.

There is minimal fencing, no asphalt unless used for trike paths, and a natural flow between interior and exterior spaces with carefully designed porches supporting this movement. Large trees are preserved. The natural setting is valued as a resource to be cherished, as an invaluable place to learn about our ecosystem, as a place of nourishment and renewal. Neither military nor industrial models are reflected here, but rather a belief that children and youth need the outside as a place where they can build, explore, relax, socialize, discover, and dream. Simply by walking into either setting, the visitor has some understanding of the vision, its history, the founders' values, and the current life style.

Striking examples of school design that reflects a particular vision are the early childhood schools of Reggio Emilia in northern Italy. These are settings where the physical environment provides a visitor with messages about the children, the importance of the physical design, the teachers and their beliefs and visions, and the daily process of learning.

> ✦*The schools in Reggio Emilia could not be just anywhere. . . . The garden, the walls, the tall windows, say this is a place where adults have thought about the quality of space . . . which reflects their personal lives, the history of the school and the immediate culture and geography of their lives.*
>
> —Gandini 1991, p. 9

The city runs 20 schools for children between three and six years old and 12 infant centers for children under three years of age. Each school is described as unique, having its own history and particular process of evolution over time. On the other hand, all schools embrace a shared vision to "create an amiable environment, where children, families, and teachers feel at ease" (Edwards et al. 1993, p. 56).

The qualities of local life in this region of Italy are reflected in the overall school plan that provides central gathering areas similar to the traditional city piazza with its porticoes and market stalls designed to support a variety of human interactions. This arrangement is a part of the vision of the Reggio educators that includes social development as essential to learning, where encounters and exchanges between children, between adults and children, and between adults may take place (Gandini 1991).

A great deal of attention is paid to details of light, beauty, and harmony. A transparent connection between the indoors and outdoors is provided by large windows, the absence of clutter, inside gardens or atriums, and many plants. "We call them gardens of beauty. They show some things of nature.

You can see the sky and trees come out of the roof" (The Children of Reggio Emilia 1993). Teachers may also put small mirrors outside on a table to enable children to experience the patterns of leaves, light, and the changing color of the trees above them (Bartlett 1993).

The vision that guides the architects, educators and families of these schools in Italy is one in which the environment is an essential part of the educational approach and must reflect the people and their interactions. Flexibility is important, allowing children and teachers to modify their environment. In this collaborative effort each school can be described as unique, a place where the vision, history, and many layers of culture are reflected (Edwards et al. 1993).

The schools of Reggio Emilia describe a fit between the built environment, the educational vision, and the users' activities. Attention is paid to the ways the environment structures and organizes social interaction and children's exploration. Environments should be arranged and rearranged according to personal preferences, the goals and values of people who use the space, and the overall vision of that particular program.

Process

◆*The beauty is in the walking*
We are betrayed by destinations
—Welsh poet Gwen Thomas (source unknown)

When design takes place over time, it is similar to a journey. Walking slowly through a town for the first time is a feast of sights, sounds, smells, and textures; the familiar and the unexpected. The way the sidewalk is uplifted by the huge roots of cottonwood trees, the delicate blue of tiny flowers surviving in cement cracks, the smell of burning piñon from a fireplace chimney, the patterns of clouds, the coolness of shade make each step a small adventure. The emphasis falls on the process—walking, not the end point—destination. Designers, teachers, and children are in a position to enjoy the walking together. There should be space for them to pause en route, opportunity for them to make choices, to absorb what is already there, to reflect and envision what might be. There should be time for them to look for road signs to clarify their route. With greater emphasis on the process of design over time, there is the opportunity to assess how a setting currently fits the behaviors of those who are using it and to predict what might happen or change. Destinations, like products, provide focus and direction to a journey but should not overshadow and dominate the process.

Teachers and children are travelers who are familiar with the journey, its past, its route, its pitfalls and problems. From time to time they need the view of the outsider to join their walk—a person who experiences it as new rather than familiar. Teachers may be blinded by routine and need to see in fresh ways the sidewalks, the flowers, the patterns of shade and sun. The designer has the training and opportunity to see in this way, to understand the many dimensions of the physical environment, to discover creative solutions that have yet to be imagined, and to approach what exists with new vision.

Designers provide expertise at different parts of a journey. Where and when the players' paths cross could be at any point en route. They might join each other at the beginning, before anything has been designed, built, or used, or in process, to improve or retrofit an existing setting. Signs that help to clarify the process are often missing. Understanding where the journey began, its past route, at which point it is currently, and what its continuing pathway might look like is important. Designers need these directional clues because they are en route only for a limited time and yet must find ways to understand the users and their space—past, present, and future. Is there flexibility to change this setting? How does time impact what has happened or might happen to physical forms? What kinds of environmental design choices have teachers made in the past and why? Who has the power to make physical changes? What changes have there been, when, and why? Why do parts of the setting seem to fit or not to fit some teachers and children?

Signs en Route

When walking through a town for the first time, a traveler often asks directions, consults a map, or looks for street signs to better understand the route. Directions may be incomplete, arbitrary, or incorrect but should provoke thinking that facilitates the journey's progress. During the process of designing outside spaces for children and youth, teachers and designers also need clues, maps, and signs to aid progress. Described in the following sections are four elements; time, flexibility, legacy, and choice. These "signs en route" are useful directional clues. The four elements impact a process of developing congruence between people and place. These "signs" are explained and then followed by case studies—illustrations of real journeys taken by young people, teachers, and designers working together. The case study settings vary from dense urban areas to rural landscapes. Public and private institutions, preschool and school age children, and contrasting cultural or religious affiliations are represented. The neighborhoods include secluded streets dominated by single-family homes, and busy thoroughfares with both residential and commercial use. A secure, predictable, vandal free environment is the primary goal for some players. Others take their safe place in the world for granted. These stories are told as descriptions, not solutions. They show a way of viewing the design process whereby a fit between users and the physical setting is the ultimate destination.

> ◆ *"Ideally a child's play space should never be finished, it should be in a constant state of change."*
>
> —Goltsman, in Shell 1994, p. 79

Time Working in a physical space over time provides adults with feedback about what works and what doesn't work. Having time allows opportunities to make choices. Adults need chances to tamper with their space, to engage in divergent thinking, and to discover results. This process includes trial and error, in which adults watch young people's behavior to understand the physical setting and how it works.

Like the changing behavior of children, the natural outdoor world of plants also develops over time. Trees eventually grow large enough to provide shade, flowers bloom adding color, foliage becomes habitats for small animals, areas decay and nourish further changes. Children interact with this natural world. Pathways emerge over time from the accumulated imprints of small running, walking, skipping feet. Shrubs become hideouts, boundaries, or, perhaps, problem areas. The evolution of both the plant material and the children impact this journey of discovery of personal "fit" over time. Congruent settings do not happen quickly.

The following case study also describes an evolution over time of an outside area—an art studio for children ages three through teens. The setting is located on the campus of Pacific Oaks Children's School in Pasadena, California. The creation of this outside art space began as a part of the artist-in-residence program supported by grants by the state of California during the late 1970s. As an early recipient of such funds in the 1970s, artist Karen Neubert was initially challenged by the grant's guidelines to create an art studio. She chose to do this outside and has been working on this environment over the past 16 years. Here is an example of a congruent setting, described by a fellow faculty member as "a quiet, secluded, beautiful space that *fits* Karen's style; it is gentle and not demanding, . . . the space is Karen." Karen tells this story as both a teacher and artist/designer; it is her process of "design over time."

CASE STUDY
The Art Studio, Pacific Oaks Children's School
Pasadena, California

✦It was full of sunshine that first day of art.
The new student, Elise, age five, came to the table,
scanning the array of collage materials there
"You can do collage outside and then go play?"

Karen:

When I first saw the area, it was a neglected back-border space along a fence—a space no one saw as useful except for the storage of stuff. Searching the campus for a suitable space for an art studio, I opened the wooden gate and saw a long view opening into a bright, wide, sky-lit space punctuated with dappled shade from two 60-foot-high eucalyptus trees. Arching over my head was a dark tunnel-like shed roof. In the middle of the open space lay a 20-foot pile of construction material. Under this heap lay 50 or more chunks of what had been a massive oak tree. Recently removed from the preschool children's yard, because of disease, this mammoth tree had artfully

The art studio: a long tunnel
that opens to the sky.
(Photo by Karen Neubert.)

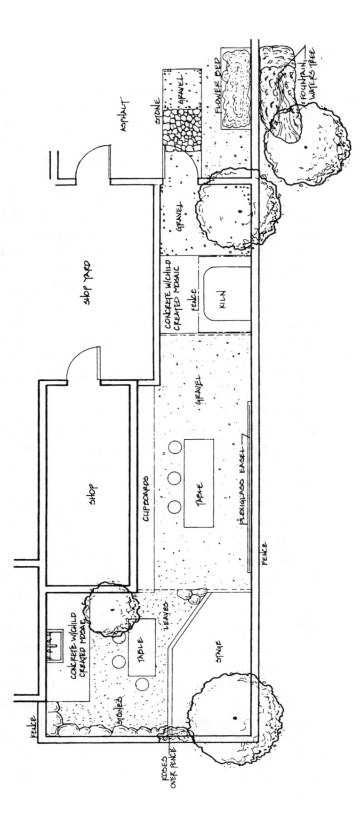

The Art Studio, Pacific Oaks Children's School.
Area before removal of large eucalyptus tree. Current design of space used by children for art activities.

twisted through a porch roof for many years. The tree, a powerful visual memory for everyone who had experienced it, now lay forgotten in pieces.

The California Arts Council required an existing studio for the artist to receive the grant. I needed a theater of operation. This space was completely enclosed, private, cool, sunny, secluded, and I felt it would work. Creation of the outside art studio began.

It was going to be a horrendous job. The first thing to go was a 1930s icebox. A yard sale was organized, where we also sold pieces of the sacred oak tree. The cupboards full of rat droppings, outdated curriculum effluvia, and moldy carpet samples were rehabilitated. We hauled out the construction debris and found the rudiments of a small deck or stage—some teacher's project, begun earlier, perhaps never finished, its importance disappearing with the adults who created it. A parent volunteered to put decking on this foundation. The only object present on our new stage between the two giant eucalyptus trees was an antique hardwood Victrola box holding a dress-maker's cloth dummy. We called it "the teacher." This assemblage, which turned clunkily around, weathered to a lovely violet gray and provoked many discussions about shape.

I cleaned out the cupboards and swept two years' accumulation of eucalyptus leaves off the shed's roof. A soft, diffused light came through the plastic roofing. I found an old table and purchased two 12-foot pieces of wood and stacked these on bricks to display children's work-in-process. We were off! The children had helped with the entire cleanup and setup process, but I knew it was beginning to work when I saw them skipping as they entered this new space for art. It was the beginning of a long, fertile period of creation.

Rain was an endless problem. The elderly plastic roofing leaked. I poured bags of pea gravel on the ground surfaces to help keep the area dry. The dirt pathway that led to the gate of the art studio was often under water. I collected large, smooth river rocks, common in this area of the Pasadena arroyo, and made a stone path leading into the studio. River rocks along the fence created a border and maintained the edge of our natural carpet of fragrant eucalyptus leaves. Flowering shrubs reseeded and burst into magenta each spring. An ant family prospered in a secluded back corner. Behind the large trees, squirrels ran along the top edge of the fence, delighting the children. The animals curiously watched us playing with clay and paint.

It took four years to get a sink installed. We improvised with buckets of water placed at strategic points throughout the space. Finally, I claimed a splendid portable sink built by a former teacher. It had two tiers, one adult

Children help decorate the sink area with shells and tiles.
(Photo by Karen Neubert.)

height, one for preschoolers and two-year-olds. A sculptor friend invented a clay trap so that we could reach in and remove clods of clay, gravel, and leaves. When the sink was connected to the plumbing system of the adjacent building, years of hauling hot water finally ended. Using shells and bits of tile, children helped create colorful mosaic patterns in the cement area around the sink.

In the heat of August 1986, during my sabbatical leave, I received a phone call. The art studio had burned to the ground, along with the kindergarten building and the old original shop building. When I arrived, it was more than 100 degrees outside. I opened the gate and saw an ashen cave, sunlight streaming through and gleaming on trailing strands of plastic roofing. Two blackened tree columns were still standing. The fence was a lacework of charcoal blisters. I was in a state of shock. Nine years of work were gone.

Passing through the roofed-over area and into the open space, I saw foot after foot of silvery, charcoal gray fencing still standing, temporarily, precariously, supported by burned nails. The ashes flew up at each step, and crunching, splintery sounds accompanied my progress through the space. In the rubble on the stage was the remains of "the teacher," now a twisted, shrunken mound of powdery white ashes and steel resting atop the old Victrola box. The destroyed art supplies were inventoried and valued. What was irreplaceably gone was the feeling—the green, the artful divisions of space into a magical garden.

After two years of conducting the art program in temporary areas, seemingly endless sessions of difficult fundraising, and convincing others of the importance of an art studio out-of-doors, rebuilding began. As the roof went up, so did my spirits, and it seemed to be a focal point of excitement for the children. The light filtered through the two new rain-tight skylights. In the past, our floor of eucalyptus leaves fell naturally into layered arrangements, pale pink, green, and violet. Children noted the fragrance when we washed down the stage and sprinkled these leaves. Since the fire we have had to garner fresh oak leaves from nooks and crannies on the edges of the school. The natural feeling doesn't simply happen; I must carefully work to create naturalness.

Disaster struck again the next year. This time its cause was natural rather than the action of an arsonist. Exceptionally hard Santana winds brought down eucalyptus tree limbs, smashing the deck and tearing apart the fence. Tree experts determined that the fire and subsequent rains had permanently damaged the eucalyptus trunks. It was decided to chop them down. We were all saddened. Our fragrant shelter was gone, the studio was barren. Attempts to level and smooth the stumps, to use them as tables or sculpture stands, failed when the massive saw blade broke because of the hardness of dead eucalyptus wood.

With help from a landscape architect, we discussed the trees and the potential future feel of this area. She noted that a volunteer fig had sprouted close to the arson spot and a Chinese elm was roof high. We were beginning to notice some dappled shade. Next to the easel was a neighbor's rose bush, its small flowers tumbling over the fence and falling to the ground like a yellow waterfall. The special quality of the space was slowly returning.

Two years later I returned after the summer break to find the kindergarten and maintenance area rebuilt. The carefully designed clerestory opening that ran the length of the art studio's covered area, providing a band of sunlight and view of distant trees, was completely obscured by this new construction. The cross ventilation was now gone, the light reduced. Design decisions were made that summer by the business office manager, rather

than according to the careful plans I had developed with an architect the previous spring. I attempted to explain the problem to a very busy trustee. His response was that the whole outside area would be wonderful when it was roofed in, more like a real classroom. My heart sank. I knew I did not want to cover up that brilliant blue sky, the circling hawks, the yellow poplar leaves, the large white blossoms on the neighbor's magnolia tree, or the distant view of seasonal purple of the jacaranda tree. I would endure the cold, the heat, the damp before sacrificing the outdoor beauty I had spent so many years conserving for the children.

I always have a vision of what this space might be. It is something like a painting, an intimately familiar process for me. I work on this environment as I work on my paintings, every day looking, making mental changes, tentatively rearranging the moveable parts, looking at the whole but in different lights, then returning the next day to see if it fits. From time to time, I seek advice about the space from fellow artists and designers who lend support, encouragement, and a sense of humor. They help me stay in touch with an overall vision when I become bogged down with the details of maintenance, of keeping the space clean and dry. They help me remember to value the importance of time in any creative process.

The outside studio will never be finished. I hope that the people who work in the space will always be adapting, creating, changing the space to make it work. Because it is out-of-doors, some changes will happen naturally over time because of sun, vegetation, and rain. As a teacher, I have been torn by the pressures to keep the art studio maintained while knowing that this is a place for children of all ages and their multifarious artworks will be messy. As an artist, I have struggled between wanting to change and redesign the space, and understanding that this takes time. On the other hand, I have felt the deadlines and constraints of needing to use the studio environment.

The art studio space has an intimate natural beauty that is nurtured.
(Photo by Karen Neubert.)

Looking back over the years of creation and destruction, I realize that I work with an interplay between natural elements. I was brought up with a love of Japanese art and landscape design. The concepts of interior and exterior, of light and shadow, of positive and negative, are vitally important in the creation of a space where the mind can be free. The distant view has been as important in my design of the outside studio as the closeup intimate view. The unique beauty of the spot and its particular character are the elements I work with. It is an active stage where children can create and a quiet spot where children and adults can experience the silent energies left behind in the fences and stones and trees.

◆ . . . *ambiguous, hidden, wild, unkempt, leftover places of childhood days.*

—Lynch and Lukashok 1956, p. 142

Flexibility   The art studio developed over a long time period in which both human intervention and natural processes influenced its form. Trees, wood, stone, dirt, flowers, and leaves shaped its environment. The materials were on site, easy to work with, inexpensive, and familiar to all the players. In analyzing outside environments for children, it is helpful to question what materials have been used and why. Are there some on-site, native, inexpensive materials that might be used? How can built forms incorporate flexibility in the types of materials that are initially selected for use?

Families who originally came over the El Camino Real from Mexico City to northern New Mexico built homes that grew with the births and marriages of their children. As the family enlarged, rooms were added. Three elements of these traditional homes support a process of change by providing flexibility. First, the materials were readily available and often on site. Adobe bricks formed walls, cedar and pine *viegas* and *latillas* shaped the ceilings, and native plants softened, added color, and shade to outdoor areas. Second, the materials were inexpensive and could be shaped by hand. People did not need to be highly trained to use them; therefore, families were not dependent on specific technologies or trained experts or people who were not a part of their community. Third, the materials were native to the area and people were familiar with them. On site, inexpensive, easy-to-use, familiar materials support flexibility to make changes.

In the case study that follows, teachers transplanted pussy willow from a neighbor's yard, used an old lemon tree—remnant of a bygone orchard, incorporated existing dirt and sand, created play spaces from old feed bins, and added a cargo net from the nearby marina. These play space building blocks, the plants, sand, and cargo net, were from the local area, easy to work with, inexpensive, and familiar to the school community. The story that unfolds describes how a play space is created where flexibility is an important ingredient.

Located in east Ventura, California, in a large middle class community on a main thoroughfare, the immediate neighborhood of Eastminister Sonshine Preschool is a mix of working and middle class families. The school is surrounded by single family homes and farms. The play areas of the school are made up of "leftover" spaces adjacent to or between buildings and parking areas of the church. Vandalism is a constant and increasing problem. The following story is told by Mary Taylor, Sonshine Preschool's founding director. Like Karen, Mary's vision originally guided and directed the pathway of this school's development. She describes the first two years, September 1983 to the spring of 1985, when selection of flexible materials was a critical part of the process of trying to fit a new preschool program into an existing church school environment. She shares her journey of creating a play yard from scratch. Mary's story is interspersed with a description of the same setting 12 years later by Pat Ringler, a teacher who still works in the school. She has provided the recent descriptions of the school's outside environment that illustrate the continuing search for congruence where material flexibility is an important sign en route.

CASE STUDY
Eastminster Sonshine Preschool, Ventura, California

Mary:

We created the play yard at Sonshine from scratch, or was it sand? Sand, grass, dirt, sun, shade, and morning dew made up our outdoor environment. The original yard was fenced with four-foot brown chain link. Flowering bottle brush and jasmine vines were planted all around to camouflage the fencing. The church's founding families had a talented bent toward the aesthetics, and we benefited from it. The fence gave the yard character while offering security from parking lot traffic and the bulldozers eating up the earth next door. There was soft new grass along the side of the building, and a tree lent shade. One old lemon tree served as a reminder of the orchards that once dominated this area of coastal California.

Children use the stump of an old lemon tree as a jumping platform.
(Photo by Mary Taylor.)

Pat: *"The old lemon tree finally gave out a year ago, and the children enjoy sitting on and jumping off the old stump."*

A teacher convinced the church to leave us a garden patch at one end of the yard. She and her kids planted pussy willow that first spring and it survived, much to our delight.

I was taking classes at the local college and received permission to dig up the pussy willow to plant a garden. It took years of adding soil amendments before we were able to grow much, but now the garden provides most of our vegetables all summer long.

The large yard had a long concrete walkway leading up to a wide bank of steps, and of course there was enough sand to draw camels from miles around. An outdoor sink, complete with drinking spout, was a handy source of water. Dollar Days at Sears, treasures gleaned from garage sales, and gifts from supportive friends provided the start-up equipment we needed to make the play yard exciting and inviting. The staff was in complete agreement that the quality of the outdoor environment was just as important as the indoor environment, and it was our goal to begin the school with, and to maintain, balanced play experiences. We had a water table, an old wooden table for artwork, a Big Wheel or two, sand toys, trucks, and three large graduated-size wooden boxes.

> The three boxes are still with us. They have been repainted many times, the edges and panels have been replaced so often they are hardly the original boxes. They get a great deal of use, the best used pieces of equipment we have.

We would haul the easel outside for painting, and by the end of the day the brown fence was gaily decorated with the children's artwork. A child's kitchen set salvaged from someone's garage made the yard complete. During the outdoor time, the long steps going up to the door became a time-out spot, a sit-down-and-rest spot, and a take-off-your-shoes-and-dump-the-sand spot. We wore out brooms sweeping the sidewalks clean and shared the unpleasant task of sifting the sand for treasures left by neighborhood cats.

We officially opened our doors in October 1983. As the year progressed, our enrollment increased and we began to get inquires for the next year. Though the play yard environment was working well, we reevaluated its offerings and decided we needed a multiplay structure. This would add diversity to the environment and provide several choices for play, as well as accommodate several children at one time. One teacher, walking around a structure, would be able to supervise the many adventures in progress. It was a time when we knew we needed some expertise in design and construction. We couldn't afford to hire someone to help us but discovered the plans of what we wanted in *Sunset Magazine*. We wanted to use simple, easy-to-work-with materials. A friend, also a preschool director, supplied the name of a carpenter who agreed to build the structure for the cost of materials plus a nominal fee. We had the climbing structure built during Easter vacation. It was a large wooden box with a fenced-in deck on top that allowed the children to see for miles. A wide ladder was the only means of assent, and an equally wide slide was the only other way down. One side of the structure had a big hole that led inside the box. This was a great hidey-hole, and it became the favorite spot for the more quiet children. A door, which could be locked open, also made this our storage space for balls, sand toys, and trucks. Support beams held a flat-side tire swing that sat three children. A cargo net we obtained from our local marina, to test children's pirating skills, pleted the square. When the cargo net finally wore out, a chin-up bar was added.

> *We modified the structure over time as parts wore out or were vandalized. It was finally beyond repair, and last spring we held fundraisers and bought a new structure similar to those designers are installing in local city parks and recreation areas. We wanted something maintenance free.*

When we had saved more money, we had a large wooden shade cover built into one corner of the yard. Art projects and mud pies were created in cool comfort.

> *That "weed" that grew between the bushes is now a tree more than 12 feet high and rests most of its branches on top of the original shade structure, doing what the structure was designed to do.*

The long walkway was the route used by the Big-Wheelers. Of course, this worked only until our enrollment increased, when more wheel toys were needed, thus creating a traffic-pedestrian safety problem. The church came to our rescue. An additional square of concrete was fenced off, creating a very large riding area. There was a gate on the opposite side of the fence that allowed access to the school from the parking lot. This was an exciting addition, because the fence kept the wheel toys completely separated from the rest of the yard, accessible by an easy-to-open gate. The bushy fence created pockets for play, separating budding artists from energetic trike riders. Riders were free to pedal away, and children waiting for a turn played outside the fence. A shade tree was planted smack in the middle of the square. The children were delighted to ride rings around the tree.

> *In 1990 we had a flat, round wooden bench built around the tree. It made an ideal place for teachers to sit and visit with children. That original tree is now so large, we had to increase the size of the bench this year.*

We began our second year with a full enrollment (36 children—three through five years of age). Staff members were eager to make full use of every square foot of the yard. Our attention turned to the grass area. We agreed that we wanted to leave this place free of any permanent equipment. We searched constantly for flexibility. There were times when everyone wanted to get away from the gritty sand and hard, hot concrete. What better oasis than the soft, shaded grass? Through mutual though unspoken consent, the grass became the place for a quieter kind of play. The free, open grass lent

The tree in the center of the wheel toy area is a place to gather.
(Photo by Mary Taylor.)

to spontaneous games, somersault tournaments, song fests, and snack-time picnics.

> *A second garden area was added at the far end of the grassy area. Previously we had a difficult time keeping grass growing here. Once we planted tomatoes, onions, and green peppers, the children were very careful not to run over the plants with their trikes.*

We purchased a bright molded plastic picnic table designed especially for little people. We never indicated any special intent for the table. The children made it their social center. A teacher discovered sturdy cardboard barrels at a feed store and encouraged the owner to donate them to us. They soon became favorite getaway spots.

> *The large cardboard tubes wore out with time and a great deal of use. We tried to get new ones, but when I explained to the Board that we would have to pay a little something for them, unfortunately the barrels were voted down even though they provided the flexible play spaces we had valued for so many years.*

*Eastminster Sonshine
Preschool.*
*Outside play yard showing
trike area, sand, storage,
and garden.*

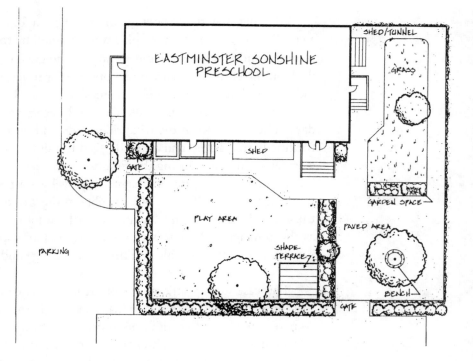

By this time we had accumulated enough outdoor supplies to keep 36 children excited, happy, and content. However, there was no outdoor storage except for the "hidey-hole." Precious time and energy were lost in hauling supplies outdoors and in again. Our next project was a storage shed. Once again we evaluated the play yard and made plans for a new addition. Obviously we did not want the storage shed to take away any play space. The long walkway up to the steps, fortunately, was extra wide. The church approved of our idea to build the storage shed against the wall, next to the steps. This was added in September of the next year. It was built flush against the wall, leaving the sidewalk clear. Wide opening doors made cleanup time a pleasant group project, as children and teachers worked together in storing the outdoor equipment.

> *I remember how creative we had to be to get even the few toys we had that first year into the hidey-hole. The shed we built for storage back then is now a bit shabby but it still serves its purpose. The roof shingles have been replaced at least once and the doors are sagging, but it was a wonderful idea that we still need and use.*

What began with the opening of the school as one huge sandlot was now a child's play haven. Areas of play were defined by the senses, as well as by activities and equipment. Sand, concrete, and grass tickled one's touch. The deck on the climbing structure let one see for miles, while the inside of the hidey-hole hid everything else from sight. The shade from the trees and overhead shelter kept one cool. The sand became a beach on warm sunny days. The squeal from the trike riders invited boisterous play, and the soft rocking barrels lulled and quieted. It's difficult to say whether the play yard ever felt complete. During the first two years, serious planning, innovative ideas, and sheer spurts of imaginary play by staff kept the environment flowing. It was a reflection of our belief in the wonders of the young child, the grit of determination to create a special outdoor place to nurture children as they change and grow with each new season, supported by an outdoor play space that was flexible and must also change and grow over time.

This case study is an example of the importance of ensuring flexibility, so that those who follow are able to make changes in the physical space. Materials were used to support a continuous process of establishing congruence between a founding vision, the built environment, and the activities of children and teachers who would continue to use the space. Flexibility, allowing them to change the spaces, was supported by easy-to-use on-site materials such as sand, dirt, shrubs, trees, flowers, and grass. Initially, small actions were required to create congruence, such as the addition of pussy willows to an existing garden patch. As the setting continued to evolve and more permanent structures were needed, flexibility remained a concern; wood was a primary construction choice. Once these structures were built, the outside space became less flexible but could still be maintained by the teachers and parents.

Designers have an opportunity to help teachers figure out what kinds of flexibility they need on their journey toward a better fit between behavior and physical design. Flexibility gives teachers more control over their settings; fixed designs exclude them from the loop of choice making. Choosing materials that are available on site, inexpensive, and easy to use helps to ensure greater flexibility, for those who follow, in readapting the setting to their particular use.

> ◆*She took me into the great hall and invited me to browse through the "storybooks." More like family albums, they were hand-crafted celebrations of the memories and meaning of the school's activities.*
> —Kinn 1989, p. 44

Legacy A congruent setting that has developed over time often becomes inflexible because of the permanence of the built forms that have evolved. For example, in a school for children two through nine years of age, teachers valued experiences with animals. Originally some small animals were kept in a variety of flexible spaces: the ducks paddled in whatever mud puddle the children made, the fences were temporary "snow fencing", the guinea pig or rabbit cages moved from yard to yard. Over time, with design assistance, a concrete duck pond was built that could be drained and cleaned. Interesting patterns of children's handprints personalized the edges. The rabbit and guinea pig cages were permanently constructed along an adjacent concrete block wall. The entire animal space was enclosed in chain link fencing, strong enough to withstand the assault of a neighborhood dog should it happen to get into the yard during the weekend. The outdoor area was a place where children learned to respect the rights of the ducks and rabbits who lived there. This daily experience with animals in their home was the vision of one particular teacher. The animal's quarters were built in her yard. She created an educational program around this physical space as she shaped it over time. It was a wonderful fit for her vision of what the kindergarten program should be for her five-year-olds. Other teachers at the school let their groups of children visit the animals' home and enjoyed the accessibility of ducks and rabbits on the site. However, with the exception of the kindergarten teacher, very few adults were willing to take responsibility for the ongoing maintenance necessary when ducks, geese, rabbits, or guinea pigs live in a schoolyard space. It was not everyone's vision, nor a space they had worked to build, or part of the way they focused their curriculum. This was a physical design that was an excellent fit for one teacher (and appreciated by others as long as they had no responsibility for its upkeep). When she no longer worked in this particular outside space, the animal yard became a legacy inherited by those who followed. Because the area was permanent and resistant to change, other teachers felt stuck with it.

Inflexible, incongruent settings will always exist in some form; however, it is important that spaces like the animal area are created, because they model the importance of a "good" fit. It is also helpful if such spaces are built with the understanding that over time the setting will probably become another person's legacy. Leftover legacies in a planned environment are even more difficult to deal with when the meaning of the particular design is lost. The intention and goals of the animal area were always clear. On the other hand, over the years no one seemed to know why the five-foot diameter ring of eight-inch raised concrete was built, what it was for, or how to use it. Located

No longer used, their meaning lost, concrete rings were built to fit the needs of a past program.

in a major school pathway, the circle was ignored, tripped over, and walked around. The story and logic of this structure was lost 15 years earlier when Grace, the teacher who had it built, retired. She valued children's group experiences. The concrete ring was a safe edge where children could sit around a campfire, experience its warmth, share songs and stories, and feel part of their group. She would tell stories, magically describing the wonder and danger of fire. Children wrote poems and sang songs, but when Grace retired, the cement ring, no longer used, lost its meaning. It became a disruptive object in everyone's way. What was once a match between a physical form and a teacher's personal style, experience, and philosophy, later became a meaningless problem area. It was a legacy of built forms difficult to change because of the use of inflexible materials.

Schools often occupy inherited spaces where the entire outside area is a legacy from an earlier program. For example, the Armenian early childhood-kindergarten program, Tufenkian School, is located on a site originally built in the 1940s as a Baptist church. Its buildings and grounds are inherited spaces designed to accommodate a Sunday only program. Located in the eastern area of downtown Glendale, a block away from the high school, the site is bordered by a major four-lane thoroughfare to the west. The community of small single family homes that surrounds the school was built during the 1940s, and two-story apartment buildings and a convenience shopping area across the street were added in the 1960s. The Baptist church site was purchased in 1976 by a group of Armenian immigrants with a strong educational vision for their children.

The Baptist church and its grounds were a physical legacy, whereas the expectations and experiences of the Armenian families and teachers were a cultural inheritance for Tufenkian School. As illustrated in the following case study, these legacies heavily impacted the change process as the director attempted to create a fit between her educational vision, the teachers' goals, and the existing physical environment.

Tufenkian School adapted buildings and outside spaces that were designed and built to house a Baptist church.

For the Armenian families at Tufenkian School, a primary means of support in maintaining their traditional culture is their educational system. A purpose of Armenian schools is to teach Armenian children to read, write, and speak their language accurately and fluently. Initially the Baptist church buildings were adapted to serve as both a school and an Armenian church for the growing immigrant population migrating to this area of southern California. Ida Karayan was hired to direct the school in 1979 and continued in this capacity for 14 years. Her story is a complex journey that involves two contrasting cultures. She describes her first impression of an inherited "parking lot" kind of space, a hard, hot, uninviting outside area with nothing for children to do. This was a large expanse of concrete with a tiny patch of Astroturf under one slide next to a classroom wall, one set of swings, and two broken tricycles. She noticed that all 120 children came outside at the same time. With very little for the children to do in this outside space, chaos was evident. Change was required, but where to begin?

CASE STUDY
Tufenkian School, Glendale, California

Tufenkian School serves children two through six years of age and offers full day care for working families. Most families plan to continue their childrens enrollment into the elementary and junior high school located on another campus. All of the teachers are Armenian, who were born in various Middle Eastern countries and immigrated to Glendale during the past 15 years. The 250 children currently enrolled in the school are ethnically Armenian, whose parents were born in a foreign land and are therefore recent immigrants to the United States. The Armenian language must be spoken by all teachers at the school throughout the day. The only exceptions are the native English-speaking teachers hired to teach English language classes.

Ida Karayan's goal was to guide an early childhood-kindergarten program that supported the language and traditions of Armenian culture, but also adapted and incorporated early childhood practices found in the United States. Decisions about the environment were impacted by both of these sometimes conflicting values. Design decisions were affected by the Armenian church regulations and its power structure, by lack of funds, and by the urban neighborhood where graffiti and vandalism were not uncommon.

The outside play space was hard, hot, and uninviting.

Sand, as a play medium, was not part of the Armenian teachers' experience in their native lands. They saw the addition of a sand area similar to building a "kitty litter box," expressing their fears that sand was dirty, full of germs, and would be tracked into the classrooms, creating more maintenance work. Therefore, Ida initially added rubber matting under the existing slide rather than sand. She involved parents in helping raise money to buy new play equipment. A parent trained in art volunteered to paint a mural on a cinder block wall. The adjacent area seemed a good location for the play structure. With the safety as the excuse for the addition of sand, this corner of the play yard developed into a colorful space with some choice of activities. Ida knew children would enjoy playing in the sand, regardless of the addition of climbing equipment. Play equipment purchased by parents also became the excuse for adding a second sand area. Because teachers felt comfortable with gardening, part of this area, adjacent to a building wall, was set aside as a space to grow vegetables. Huge pumpkins and zucchini delighted both staff and children. Eventually teachers began to realize that the children were busier and arguing less over the limited equipment. Many children became involved in sand exploration, and teachers added buckets and shovels over

Rubber matting was initially used under slides because of teachers' concerns about the mess sand might create.

time. To keep it clean, teachers sprinkled the sand areas with water and inadvertently created more complex sand play for their children.

By 1986 the school had doubled in enrollment; however, the outside play area remained the same size overall. Assessment of the physical environment was critical; a comprehensive plan had to be developed for the outside area. A landscape architect was hired to help. To better understand the philosophy and cultural background of the school, the designer interviewed individual teachers. They were questioned about their childhood homes, their memories of play activities, and their early school experiences. This legacy offered a better understanding of what a "good" fit might mean for the staff. Their descriptions of childhood experiences were strikingly similar even though the twelve teachers grew up in different countries, which included Iran, Lebanon, Syria, and Israel. They had all attended Armenian preschools and kindergartens in their native lands. None of their schools had carpeting in as much as it was believed to be dirty. All schools had tile, stone, or cement floors. No schools had grass. With the exception of one slide and one merry-go-round, no play structures were described except swings. Outside play yards were characterized as hard surfaced, fenced areas where the children played jump rope, hopscotch, and ball games.

These descriptions of Armenian early school environments had much in common with Tufenkian School, where the hard outside space was

Children eat outdoors in the shade of trees.

bordered by classroom buildings and chain link fencing. The Glendale school was a sea of cement, white, hot, and flat, with only one tree to provide relief from the brilliant southern California sun and frequent unpleasant smog. In contrast, however, teachers recalled homes with lovely gardens and large shade trees where they played outside during their childhood. The natural beauty of the countryside was described with longing and fondness. Play among flowers, fruit, vegetables, and sometimes fountains (a Persian legacy) was remembered vividly and compared with the hard urban environment children currently experienced in the Los Angeles area. The teachers unanimously regretted what they perceived as a serious lack of natural spaces for this new generation of children growing up in Glendale. They also realized that children were spending a majority of their time in child-care settings rather than their homes because both parents had to work. They worried about these children living in a harsh and often unsafe urban area, so unlike the environments of their own childhood, where they had free time to play at home and in neighborhoods. In their native lands, safety and security were not at issue. They wanted this new generation of Armenian children to experience some of the beauty and joy they recalled but were fearful of making changes in the school's outside space that might threaten the predictability they valued at Tufenkian School. However, teachers' fond memories and concerns provided an image for physical changes to Tufenkian schools' outside play-ground that were congruent with those things teachers valued from their own childhood.

The initial design focused on removing concrete and adding plant material. Ten fast-growing trees were planted throughout the outside area. Flower- and fruit-producing shrubs were located along the chain link fence. The tree trunks and new shade patterns created different outside space configurations. There were now places to circle on trikes, places to sit and eat snacks or lunch, and places to put small plastic pools in the summertime for water play. To create comfortable shady spaces near the classrooms, awnings were added. The bright blue color of the canvas was a needed contrast to the overpowering white concrete surfaces. Like the trees, the awnings defined new outside areas. These spaces adjacent to the classrooms provided teachers with shade, where they could set up messy activities such

Trees create spaces where children can circle on wheel toys and find shelter from the summer sun.

as finger painting. When teachers seemed reluctant to set up art experiences outside, Ida hired a special part-time art teacher to provide activities of this kind for the children and to model a different use of outside space for the teachers while relieving them of the burden of changing their curriculum. It was a beginning use of the outside environment in a new way.

Because the focus was on the need for shade and the initial changes were made only in the overhead area with the addition of awnings and trees, teachers were still in charge of setting up their own outside activities on the ground. Some of the staff moved painting easels out-of-doors, while others sat with children at tables under the awnings and trees to eat snack or lunch. However, most teachers continued to use the outside area as a place primarily for physical activities for children, to "let off steam," so they could attend to the difficult Armenian and English language lessons when inside. Outdoors, everyone was more comfortable during the hot weather; the schoolyard became more congruent in this respect. Plants and awnings were a start in

Added bright blue awnings create a shady area for outside table activities.

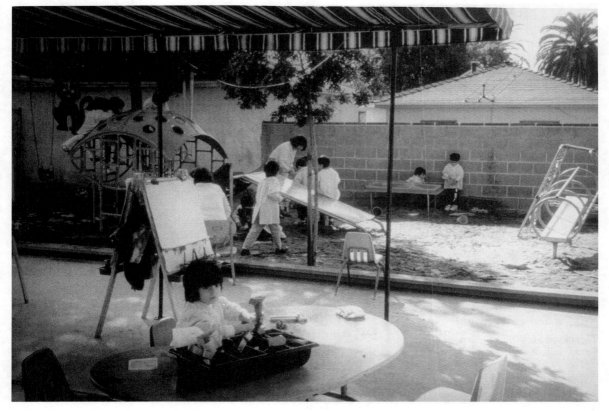

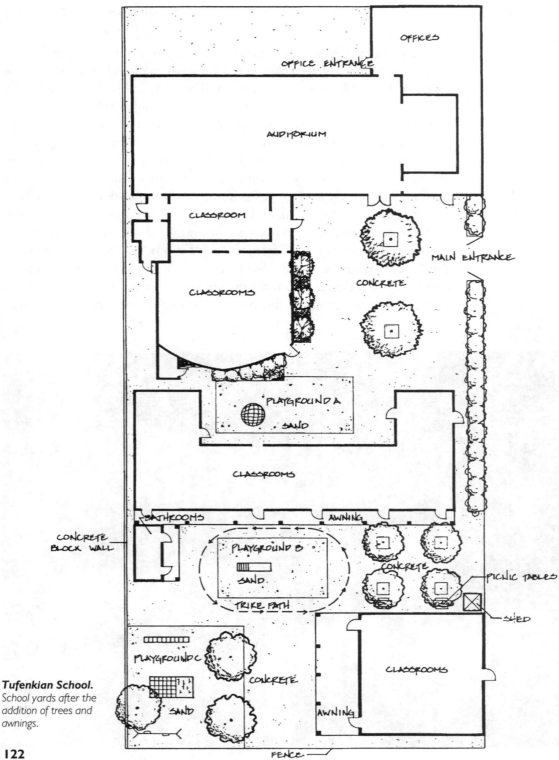

Tufenkian School.
School yards after the addition of trees and awnings.

OFFICES

OFFICE ENTRANCE

AUDITORIUM

CLASSROOM

CLASSROOMS

CONCRETE

MAIN ENTRANCE

PLAYGROUND A

SAND

CLASSROOMS

BATHROOMS

AWNING

CONCRETE BLOCK WALL

PLAYGROUND B

SAND

CONCRETE

PICNIC TABLES

TRIKE PATH

SHED

PLAYGROUND C

CONCRETE

CLASSROOMS

SAND

AWNING

FENCE

122

shaping the outside space. Now children and adults could also choose quiet activities. With help from an outsider trained in design, Ida was gently leading her teachers in the first steps of a journey to see the outside environment as a special place for many different kinds of play and exploration, at the same time working with the powerful legacy of the physical setting and the belief system of the community.

> ◆*The lowest panes of his schoolroom windows were whitewashed,*
> *when he first arrived, but he washed the paint off.* . . . *"I do what I can*
> *so that they will truly see and know the island, its soils, beaches,*
> *birds, flowers, all the transient things."*
> —Hansen, in Olwig 1991, p. 5

Choice Our adult days are filled with making choices, decisions, points in time when we have some control over some thing. The clothes we wear, the food we eat, the times we laugh and when we sleep are choices we tend to take for granted and are influenced by how we feel, by what we think we need. Choices about physical spaces are made less often as the daily routine of our lives unfolds. Environments encountered outside our home, for example, the commercial world, are usually accepted as is. We may request a specific table at a restaurant, but in general people sit where they are guided by whoever is in charge. Use or avoidance of an area is one way we make a choice or exert control over the spaces we use. This may affect economic issues but seldom impacts physical design. When avoidance of an unpleasant environment is impossible, we simply endure it; parking lots are prime examples. Making changes to a physical environment beyond our personal space is seldom within our control. And yet it is by having choice-making opportunities that teachers and designers help settings to become more congruent. If a setting is not congruent, and people who work there believe they must endure the resulting problems, then nothing will be changed. If people believe a setting is someone elses territory, that a person or group has control, change seldom happens. If these perceptions are not operating, however, there are factors that influence our behavior, motivate us to change a physical setting, to make a choice. First, some spaces are seen as physically incomplete—we move a chair on to an empty balcony. Second, if the space is not clearly defined as the territory of a particular person, group, or establishment, we are more willing to do something—we add an umbrella to the sandy area by the ocean. Third, when experimentation with the physical space is already happening—we see others making changes that improve the space, adding chairs and bringing umbrellas—we may feel we have permission do the same. Incomplete settings, areas that are not clearly defined as the territory of others, and the actions of others to change a space—all support choice making to adapt settings to better meet our needs.

For example, a corner of a certain shared schoolyard consisted of large trees, a sand area, a swing, and a dirt surface. The space was undeveloped; it felt incomplete. Children seldom used the area. The corner was not the specific jurisdiction of any particular program or teacher, and everyone complained about the lack of things to do in that space. Teachers began to take action. They used cable spools, ladders, boards, and boxes to build an apparatus for the children to explore physically. The arrangement of the climbing materials frequently changed. Together, teachers and children made daily choices about how the play area should be put together. The locus of control over this space seemed to rest with everyone who used the yard. Over time, a large permanent cable spool structure was designed and built. There was no longer a choice about how to set up the yard. The physical setting once viewed as incomplete, no one's particular territory and a place of experimentation, permanently changed with this addition. The locus of control shifted from the group to the particular teacher who had envisioned the permanent structure. It was even named after her—"Mary's Habitat." The opportunity for other teachers and children to make choices about the outside environment had narrowed.

It is easier for a setting to be congruent for the person who exerts control over the space. When others believe it is a special creation or territory of one person, they seldom advocate change to better match their own needs. If the locus of control is narrow, it is helpful for a designer to join the group as a neutral party. In this role, he or she may facilitate communication about who controls the space and why. During this process with the designer, teachers may decide that it is in the best interest of the program for the area to be primarily controlled by one person—to fit their vision. On the other hand, staff might be encouraged to engage in a process of "letting go" of control of the space to facilitate experimentation by others.

Letting Go

For me, it is a life issue. In order for letting go to be real, you have to have some kind of stake, you have to stand to lose something you care about, it is letting go of control. I remember several lessons in letting go that have stayed with me from childhood. When I was six my uncle, who was a pilot and who used to bring me giant weather balloons and coconut-heads and who was altogether very special to me, got married. He came to visit with his new wife, who was from Peru. She turned out to be very special also—warm, fun and exotic. She read to me in an accent I couldn't always understand but which I loved. When it came time for them to leave, I somehow managed to lock my new aunt in the bathroom and put the key down the toilet in the other bathroom. Unfortunately, I failed to flush the toilet, and my grandmother retrieved the key and released my aunt, so that my aunt and uncle were able to depart, more or less on schedule. It was very sad, and I ended up feeling foolish. . . . I'm still learning that you can't lock people in bathrooms to keep them where you want them. . . . The need to let go of people, turn loose of my pride, to relinquish being right—is too important to face . . . without some practice.

—Fite 1983, pp. 9–10.

When an educational setting is in a process of becoming congruent, it is important for the locus of control to rest with a wide range of potential users. At this point in the journey, there are more opportunities to choose, the flexibility to experiment and change, and the possibility that many different points of view may take part in and impact decision making. Teachers and designers need to realize that what is built, like the concrete duck pond, fire ring, or spool play structure, may occupy a space for a long time. Changing built forms can be difficult Therefore, the other adults who also work there, and those who follow, will have less opportunity to play with the space and to enjoy the process of creating congruence for themselves.

The creation of the Santa Fe Children's Museum is an example of collaborative planning, in which the locus of control has been shared among various people: designer, directors, staff, families, and children. The museum's journey is a story of four educators who had some wonderful ideas, their work with a designer captivated by this vision, and children, who could be counted on to provide input that sets everyone thinking in new ways. The museum brings together many community members who serve in advisory capacities or volunteer in the program. There is also active involvement with public and private schools in the area.

The museum is located on the Old Pecos Trail, a historical road leading to the town's plaza core in Santa Fe, New Mexico. Envisioned by four educators, it is a realization of their shared dream to create a space where children learn through active exploration and open-ended play. These women felt that the city of Santa Fe needed to offer something special and different for its children and youth, both residents and visitors. The founders also envisioned an alternative to the traditional public school educational experiences. They wanted to create a physical environment with both inside and outside spaces that supported creative thinking and problem solving for all ages.

Although Santa Fe is well known in the arts through its operas, galleries, chamber music festivals, and museums, there were no community programs designed and built specifically for children of all ages. The process of developing a children's museum as a new community project began in the early 1980s with brainstorming sessions. The museum founders recalled their years of teaching and envisioning what a special place for children might look like. They agreed that this imaginary place would support children's learning through play and active exploration. These ideas were set into motion on a small scale by creating hands-on exhibits in different locations in the community, such as in the central court area of the local mall. Schools were invited to visit and to participate. These exhibit/activities grew in number and scope. During the summers the dream of a children's museum became more than just an idea, but a temporary open air tent structure on the grounds of a well-known folk art store. Tremendous community support was generated from these "hands-on" beginnings as adults saw the need for a permanent museum space where young people could freely experiment, create, or simply encase their entire bodies in soap bubbles!

CASE STUDY
Santa Fe Children's Museum, Santa Fe, New Mexico

The story that follows is told by Londi Carbajal, one of the founding directors, and designer Jeff Harner who worked with staff, community and children in the redesign of a warehouse and the adjacent outside areas which are currently the home of the Santa Fe Children's Museum. Incorporated in 1983, this museum opened in its permanent space in February 1989. It actively serves the Santa Fe community of children, their families, and many out-of-town visitors and tourists.

Londi tells of the excitement when the state of New Mexico offered to lease at, one dollar per year, an old warehouse space to permanently house the museum. This space, an empty barnlike structure, was a part of the Armory for the Arts complex but had not been used for a number of years, except for storage. The large, open 5,000-square-foot room was dominated by accumulated dirt, debris, and darkness, but filled with possibilities in the eyes of the four museum founders. The high exposed metal beams in an open truss ceiling was a reminder of a favorite childhood place—a roller skating rink—that Londi loved. As they brainstormed ideas of just how they might transform this warehouse, the women realized that they needed professional help. It was agreed that something more should be done with the physical environment than slapping on a coat of paint, paving over dirt for a parking area, and enclosing the site with a chain link fence. What they needed was the creativity and vision of a trained professional—a designer.

It was important to hire a designer who could see the possibilities of this physical environment, who could help create a place both inside and outside to fit the vision they had been developing over the years. With this in mind, they asked all applicants a key question, "Can you work with a group of people of many different backgrounds and values and incorporate children's ideas?" In the selection process, all four finalists responded positively to this question. However, according to Londi only Jeff creatively and concretely demonstrated his understanding of the question's meaning. For inspiration, Jeff borrowed some friends' children for a day's activity. Exploration in a children's museum, he assumed, would involve water. He also knew that in designing for children, bathroom spaces are critical. Therefore, tile, as a material, might be important in this project. Jeff set up a tile making activity for these "borrowed" children in a local artist friend's studio. Unique child designed pieces of tile art were part of the package Jeff presented to the Board during his interview. This was a special response to the question as to whether, as a designer, Jeff would incorporate children's ideas. He demonstrated how he shared the values that the museum should be interactive and that the design process should involve the community. The Board felt that he understood the unique constraints of this design problem. Children's involvement would be integral to the whole design process. The Santa Fe Children's Museum would not be something mass produced, something devoid of meaning.

Because the women who envisioned the museum had been working together for the past eight years in temporary locations, a well-developed program was in place by the time a permanent physical space was offered. Communication of this vision to the designer was not a major problem. What Jeff brought to the process was his concern that the entire warehouse, both inside and outside, function as one system—an interactive environment where children and adults could experience the joy of discovery.

A major design problem with the warehouse was the 24-foot-high facade on the entry side of the building. This was definitely not at a child's scale nor

The Children's Museum's inside space is connected with greenhouse glass cube structures that break up the overwhelming feel of the exterior facade.

welcoming to families. Jeff again borrowed some friends' children, and together they made a visit to the warehouse. He encouraged them to talk about their images of this place, how they wanted to enter, where they might go when they got inside, what they would like him to build. He describes hanging out with the wonderful kid ideas, listening to the children talk about the building, watching how they walked through the space, and noting what they did with what was already there. They described a different kind of entrance, for example, a ladder that led up into the ceiling. They talked consistently about secluded places, a corner that is cozy, that is "my" space, way up high, where you can see everything but adults don't fit. They wanted a small special "kids only" kind of hideout. Londi and Jeff were getting a much clearer idea of the children's vision of their future museum.

To further focus on children's ideas, an architect in training (a previous museum volunteer) offered to work with community elementary school classes. She engaged school-age children in their classroom, creating dioramas of what a special children's museum (place) might look like. These three-dimensional art projects illustrated many ways a child might visualize entering his or her space. A repeating entrance theme was by sliding down something, like the throat of a dinosaur. The way they actually enter a physical space seemed to be important to the children. The physical forms they might need as they move into the warehouse structure should, therefore, reflect the fact that this place is for children who happen to be smaller, more agile than adults, and who enjoy physical motion.

Although Jeff and Londi were not looking for design ideas from children, such as dinosaurs, they took seriously the concerns the children expressed through their fanciful images. Children described how important it is to feel safe when you walk into a large space. They wanted to call the space their own. They wanted the entire route from the parking lot to the entrance to be a playful pathway. They wanted elements that fit only their bodies, their shorter height, their muscular abilities. Jeff describes the challenge of incorporating these concerns as he worked to change the existing overwhelming 24-foot warehouse facade that greeted visitors as they moved from the parking lot to the interior space. Unlike Alice, who changed her body size by drinking a magic potion to enter a world of Wonderland, young visitors find this warehouse entrance physically altered to fit and thus invite them. One way this was partially accomplished was by building a separate entrance with a child-size door tucked to one side of the adult-scaled entrance doors.

Jeff wanted the architecture to be playful. He deliberately left the building's structure, including heating, cooling, and water systems, exposed. One of four supporting posts on an outside overhead structure is purposely missing. Thus the building itself becomes part of a large interactive exhibit that shows how things work, raising questions for museum visitors of all ages. Jeff and Londi emphasize that there is no separation of the architecture and the museum's program goals.

A major problem outside the museum was the limited street visibility owing to the location of the structure behind another building. The ability to draw people into the museum as they drive along the Old Pecos Trail is difficult. The original land lease for the Children's Museum included only a 15-foot wide strip from the parking lot to the entrance. This limited easement area is used for circulation to and from the museum. However, Londi firmly believes that "a Children's Museum without an outdoor space is only half a museum"; therefore, developing the outside space, no matter how small, was a priority. Children expressed a desire to have fun along an entrance pathway. Trips from a car to a destination are usually a boring kind of "drag along" and "be careful" journey for children. Therefore, it was planned that from the time children and adults leave their car in the parking lot, there would be things to explore safely. These "things" are visible landmarks from the window of a passing car. Along the entrance pathway are two five-foot diameter bright purple dish-shaped structures that stand in contrast to the earth-colored landscape of northern New Mexico. A child en route to the museum can talk in front of one dish and his or her voice is easily heard by a partner 30 feet away in front of the second dish. Other outside features change with the different inside exhibits. For example, a puppet peeks out from its small theater curtain to chat with an entering child, or a wall makes interesting sounds as children strike it in different ways, or the resident parrot may be perched outside the entrance, munching its fruit and nuts. Children are invited to discover and explore along the playful little-people-oriented pathway. This museum begins outside.

During the years after the museum first opened, Londi and staff worked hard to obtain the acre of land immediately south of the building adjacent to the parking lot. Acquiring this vacant lot and receiving a grant to develop it happened simultaneously in 1992. The dream of developing the outside space as a part of the entire program began to be a reality. They would no longer feel there was only "half of a museum." Jeff, along with community volunteers with expertise in gardening and landscape design, became a part

Water from the inside play area flows outside via kid-powered pumps.

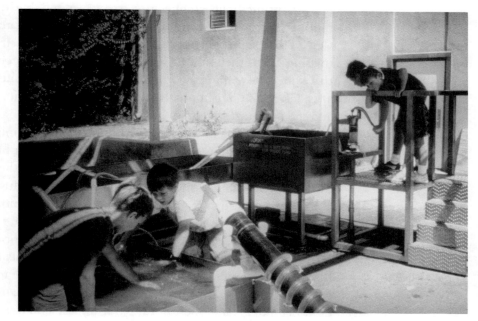

of an advisory committee to develop a site plan. Their goal was to develop a framework that would connect inside space and building forms with outside space and nature. There was an effort to make sure that the building and its adjacent outside area work as a whole, for instance, water flowing through a maze of cement channels inside the museum leads to plastic channels and a pump that invite water exploration outside. Water run-off from the museum's roof and property is collected, channeled through the wetland zones, filtered naturally, and transported to a holding tank via solar-powered and kid-powered pumps.

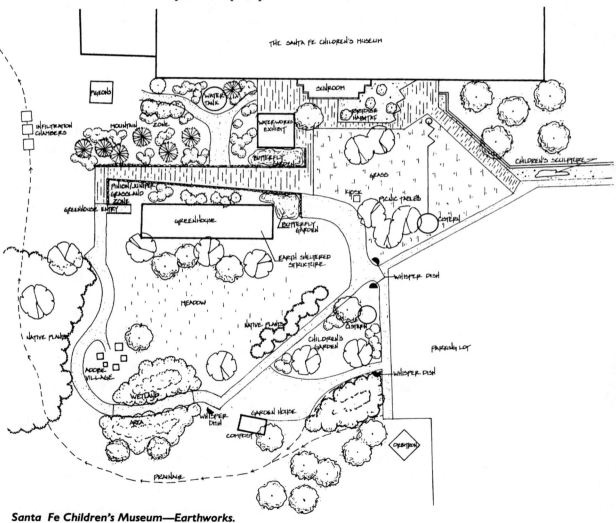

Santa Fe Children's Museum—Earthworks.
Exploratory outside environment currently under development.

An earth sheltered greenhouse is part of the museum's outside environment.

Young people dig adobe to build a small model of a northern New Mexican village in the museum's Earthworks outside activity area.

A pathway from the outside water area leads down to a greenhouse where children grow native plants for a garden. Butterfly gardens, corn and bean fields, insects and birds continually enrich this outside space. Children cart adobe soil to the greenhouse and shape it into small building bricks, at ⅛-inch scale, for an early New Mexican village they are building outside. Trails are being developed so that children will continue their exploration outside by walking through a number of locally occurring environments that include a wetland, a high desert zone, and a low desert zone. The entire outside area, known as Earthworks, is designed to involve children in hands-on projects to help them understand the uniqueness of northern New Mexico and its many ecosystems. Strategically placed signs invite exploration in this outside area.

The museum environment, both inside and outside, is seen as something organic where people respond to the overall design of the building and the land, the changing museum activities, and the people who work there. Londi believes that the environment must help visitors of all ages to feel both safe and enlightened. Overdesigned spaces, Londi and Jeff believe, result in boredom and cause people to ask, "We've seen this, so now what do we do?" What is needed instead is flexibility to make changes, add new elements, and experiment with both the inside and outside spaces over time.

Londi explains that the museum shouldn't be a space just for kids; Adults are invited to relax or to explore too. Comfortable adult-scale places to sit are integrated into the overall design, and soothing sound of water is pleasurable to adults as well as children. No signs or graphics remind parents what they should do or need to understand or explain to their child. The

At ⅛-inch scale, the village being built by children is part of the outside environment.

theme is freedom, where no one is compelled to teach or to learn, and yet this is what is constantly happening. Adults often go outdoors and lie on the grass, enjoying the comfort of being in the cool shade while their children safely explore.

As the design and program of the museum continues to unfold, Jeff maintains a relationship with the staff. He is available, on call, to help teachers and volunteer staff make design decisions, to listen to their descriptions of what is working or not working in the spaces, to simply answer their question, "Well, what do you think?" Here the players—children, educators, and designer—are in an ongoing process of making a particular space that fits.

Conclusion

The preceding case studies describe the unique journeys of educators and designers who were guided by a vision of what they believed to be important for children's learning. Each setting presents a different set of problems to solve initially and in process. The art studio was located in a neglected area of the school campus, where many years of delayed maintenance and natural and human caused disasters impacted the design and form of this special outside area. Time was a major factor in the evolution of this space. Sonshine preschool, as a new program, was faced with carving a children's outdoor

Outside exploration at the museum is as important to the staff as activities set up inside.

area from of an existing landscape. The use of local materials that were easy to change and familiar to the school community supported an ongoing process of change. Flexibility in the overall design of the outside space was important, so that teachers who followed could keep and repair or replace existing structures. The Armenian school experienced rapid growth in its enrollment, and teachers had neither the time nor resources to plan or to change the concrete area they inherited. Understanding the limitations of this built legacy and the cultural background of the teachers was of prime importance in making physical changes that supported the director's vision for the educational program. The Children's Museum is continually shaped by various groups of people, including the young people who are its primary users. They work together to shape the spaces by making choices. Input from many sectors of the community is actively sought in order to broaden the locus of control over the ways the museum space is planned and developed. Time, flexibility, legacy, and choice are elements that educators and designers can use as helpful clues to facilitate the planning and building of congruence in outside educational play spaces.

The case studies illustrate the importance of discovering directions by understanding the signs en-route. What things at this site have not changed over time, are still here, and why? What is missing outside but remembered by the people who work here? What kinds of materials are used? Do they provide flexibility to change the setting in the future? Where are the built or natural elements that tell stories, represent visions of various people? What elements provide a sense of this community, a linking of past to present for those who use this setting? Are there places that have meaning or have lost meaning? Are there areas that should not be changed, that are unique to this site and program? Who controls the space, why, how? Is there collaborative planning? What is the vision for this space and where does it come from? Sensitivity on the part of teachers and designers to these questions will help keep their journey progressing with "beauty in the walking" so that the environments that result "reflect their personal lives, the history of the school, the immediate culture and geography of their lives" (Gandini 1991).

References

Adams, Eileen. 1993. "School's out!: New initiatives for British school grounds." *Children's Environments*. 19(2): 180–191.

Alexander, Christopher. 1979. *A Timeless Way of Building*. New York: Oxford University Press.

Barker, Roger. 1968. *Ecological Psychology*. Palo Alto, CA: Stanford University Press.

Bartlett, Sheridan. 1993. "Amiable space in the schools of Reggio Emilia: An interview with Lella Gandini." *Children's Environments*. 10(2): 113–126.

Children of the Reggio Emilia. 1993. "Children in Reggio Emilia look at their school." *Children's Environments*. 10(2): 126–129.

Edwards, Carolyn, Lella Gandini, and George Forman, eds. 1993. *The Hundred Languages of Children*. Norwood, NJ: Ablex Publishing Corporation.

Fite, Karen. 1983. "'Tis a gift to be simple: Reflections on administration." In *Administration: A Bedside Guide*, edited by S. Stine. Pasadena, CA: Pacific Oaks College.

Gandini, Lella. 1991. "Not just anywhere: Making child care centers into 'particular' places." *Children's Environments* 19(2): 154–158.

Kinn, Chris. 1989. "Ingredients for a living school." *Children's Environments Quarterly* 6(1): 44–45.

Lynch, Kevin. 1981. *A Theory of Good City Form*. Cambridge MA: MIT Press.

Lynch, Kevin, and A. Lukashok. 1956. "Some childhood memories of the city." *Journal of the American Institute of Planners* 22(3): 142–152.

Moore, Robin. 1995. "Children gardening: First steps towards a sustainable future." *Children's Environments* 12(2): 222–231.

Olwig, Kenneth R. 1991. "Childhood, artistic creation, and the educated sense of place." *Children's Environments Quarterly* 8(2): 4–17.

Shell, Ellen Ruppel. 1994. "Kids don't need equipment, they need opportunity." *Smithsonian* 25(4): 79–86.

5

$\diamond \diamond$

CONTRAST

INTRODUCTION

As a third generation American of Japanese descent, I have been educated in American public schools. Not unlike a small number of other Americans of Asian and European heritage, while attending public school I also attended my grandparent's language school on Saturdays. "Japanese School" was one-third study, one-third play, and one-third confusion. The ambivalence and uncertainty generated by reading and learning about American society one day and then that of my grandparents the next, had its moments.

As a member of a minority group and raised as a minority but educated by a dominant culture, I have experienced contrast as a source of anxiety, frustration, and confusion. On the other hand, it has also been a source for reflection, recognition of choice, and assembling of inner order and a worldview.

Contrasts provide a means for understanding our decision-making process. I think this subject is critically important. Designers need to think about cultural differences and must not be afraid to get involved with them. We can utilize, in our design solutions, situations that cause us to pause and question our particular worldview.

—KEN NAKABA

Everybody needs a good cultural opposite. We learn by making comparisons, and the royal road to understanding our own way of life takes us to where we can begin to see it as others do.
—Plath 1980, p. 20

Cultural Opposites

As we seek to understand the creation of settings for children, it helps to find a "cultural opposite" (Shigaki 1983) that creates a contrast to predictable educational settings in the United States. Japan provides a contrast even though it is also a major industrial democratic nation. A key difference is the homogeneity of the Japanese people, where built forms may span a 2,000-year-old history and preschools may be located on the grounds of and in conjunction with Buddhist temples that have been in the same families for 23 generations. Although early childhood program regulations and courses of study were not published by the Japanese Ministry of Education until the late 1940s, the values underlying these programs are rooted in Japanese culture and the homogeneity of its people over an extensive period of time. Therefore, Japanese educational programs form an important contrast to those in the United States (Ishigaki 1991). A better understanding of the Japanese use of space in programs for children provides a comparison to sensitize designers and teachers in this country to the ways they design and use outside educational environments.

My thinking about outside environments for children was challenged in new ways when I was invited to spend time in Japan teaching about early childhood environments at a small junior college. My work included a varied array of visits to Japanese kindergartens (preschool age) and day care settings. To facilitate inquiry, a young Japanese woman fluent in English accompanied me to most of these site observations on the island of Kyushu, the location of the junior college. Other visits took place on the main island of Honshu, in the area of Nagano in the Japanese Alps, and in the general urban areas of Tokyo and Kyoto. An American immigrant teacher who teaches English in the Nagano schools and a Japanese member of the International Association for the Child's Right to Play (IPA) were extremely helpful during these visits. Connections and friendships forged through subsequent trips to Japan have continued to enrich my understanding of the subtle differences between the educational environments in our countries. Watching children and teachers in outside play spaces caused a reexamination of my assumptions about the ways in which physical space supports children's learning through play. We have all learned by questioning our differences. None of the following descriptions are meant to be an expert assessment of Japan's educational system, nor can it be assumed that one preschool is representative of others in the nation (Tobin, Wu, and Davidson 1989). Instead, what follows are simply personal stories, presented to spark thinking about educational environments in different ways. In the human past, skilled storytellers were our teachers, honored people who painted pictures that provided links and challenges to our understanding of why, who, or what. It is hoped that the pictures painted here in the spirit of storytelling also challenge the reader's thinking.

Kyushu, Japan   As the train travels south of the city of Fukuoka, on the Japanese island of Kyushu, the landscape is rich with small farms, vegetable plots, and rice paddies. The pace seems slower, the towns smaller, and the massive scale of Tokyo's high-rise structures and the streetscape crush are a world apart. Located in this rural farming area is Otani Junior College, a Shinshu Buddhist school, part of Kyoto Otani University, founded in 1665. A junior

Rice fields lie adjacent to a school in a rural area of Kyushu, Japan.

college in Japan can be described as half a university—two rather than four years of study, three major departments rather than six or seven. Otani Junior College offers courses in three areas of study: Japanese literature and language—which includes the study of library sciences, theater and broadcasting; early childhood education; and Buddhism.

Of the 380 students who attend, approximately three-fourths are enrolled in the early childhood education program. Students are predominantly female, between the ages of 18 and 22. After completion of this two-year course of study, it is expected that they will teach in one of the kindergarten programs or day-care facilities in this rural area of Japan. It is also expected that after these young women marry, at about the age of 26, they will leave teaching and devote their full-time energies to raising a family. Although this traditional view of women as primarily homemaker is changing in Japan, Kyushu, remote from the major urban centers, is still heavily influenced by many generations of traditional Japanese culture.

Kyushu Otani Yochien is a lab school program, located on the college campus. The preschool provides training for the young women studying early childhood education. Known in Japan as a kindergarten rather than a preschool, Kyushu Otani Yochien serves 180 children who are three, four, and five years old. There are eight separate classes, each with its own inside physical space and shared outside area. Student teachers spend a great deal of time observing the children, who come from families in the surrounding community. Families pay a set amount, but the state and national governments finance 20 percent of the budget. All Japanese kindergartens are funded in this way. The separation of support for private schools is different from that found in the United States.

The organizational ties between Kyushu Otani Yochien and the college are very strong. For example, although the lab school has a separate board of trustees, its members are all Otani College faculty members. The school is directed by a college professor, known as the president, and this position usually rotates every two or three years among the faculty. Positions of leadership in day care, kindergartens and elementary schools in the Japanese educational system are usually held by men.

The case study that follows is narrated by Mary Beth Lakin, an early childhood professor who spent two years working at Kyushu Otani Junior College. She and her husband made their home in an on-campus college apartment. This extended stay enabled Mary Beth to move beyond her powerful first impressions, to look beneath the surface, to continually ask questions in order to better understand Japan's early childhood programs.

CASE STUDY
Kyushu Otani Yochien, Chikugo, Kyushu, Japan

> *Immersion in another person's reality, coming to it without preconception, accepting it for what it is, was such a simple act; the main difficulty was one of getting into the act, of being able to drop roles, titles, and mutual expectations, and find a neutral meeting ground. . . . Designers need to take the simple step of going out and meeting people in their own habitat . . . in their own physical setting, . . . [with] the actual stuff of a person's life.*
>
> —Moore 1990, p. xvii

Mary Beth:

Living in Japan, especially in the rural area of Kyushu, was an important experience for me. It told me how I approach the environment and what I do in an unfamiliar one. It helped me to understand how culture informs my sense of place. I grew up in the 1950s in a middle class white neighborhood in the southern area of the United States. Moms stayed at home; kids rode bikes around the block, played baseball in a friend's backyard, sledded down the steep street in the winter, swung across a creek on a muscadine vine in the summer, and spent endless hours in the sandbox, making and sampling mud pies. My childhood was influenced by the climate, terrain, space, vegetation, seasons, and Southern culture. I learned that our culture influences how we organize our space and how we live together in a particular climate. As someone who grew up in a small town in the humid South, I understand why Southerners may move at a slower pace. The climate and the culture demand it.

In the beginning of my two year stay in Japan, I was looking for a way to fit into the Japanese culture. My approach was to look at the physical setting and let this provide cues about what I might be required to do. For example, I frequently found myself in homes that were traditionally Japanese, which meant sitting at a low table on pillows. In these situations, I observed how to sit down, what to do with my legs, and where to put my feet. After a few times, I made sure to pay attention to how the women of my age were sitting, as age and gender matter. I quickly learned the translation of "please relax," which meant that I no longer needed to sit with my legs carefully tucked under my body, but could assume a position much easier for a Westerner. I carefully searched for physical evidence in the environment that would help me understand expected behavior such as where to put my shoes, how to eat various foods, what to do with a dripping umbrella, where to get on the bus, and when to change footwear. These physical and visual signs and the thoughtfulness of friends and colleagues helped me understand how to behave.

Japan, for me, was a place of unrecognizable sights and smells—neon kanji, hiragana and katakana, varieties of fish I'd never seen or smelled, conversations in which as a beginner in Japanese language, I usually understood only every fifth word. Japan seemed dark and closed in, especially because I had lived for the previous 10 years in southern California, with its expansive skyline and pastel colors. I felt closed in by the somber colors of the buildings and homes and furnishings. These contrasts to my past experiences, the feelings engendered by many inside spaces, helped me to understand how culture informs our sense of place.

However, there was also familiarity in the Japanese environment. The warm, humid climate, the proliferation of plants and insects, the seasonal changes, the hilly and green terrain—all reminded me of my childhood home in the South. The outdoors, especially away from many of the signs of "civilization," made me feel at home—in my childhood. Although the indoor spaces were often confusing and constraining, when outside I felt a sense of comfort, a sense of the familiar.

I found the outside play environment, at the lab school in the college were I was teaching, unexpectedly rich in the ways the children are able to explore their natural world. There is an abundance of dirt, sand, water, and plants, but a complete absence of asphalt, concrete, and chain link fencing. A large sand area is equipped with plastic shovels, buckets, and watering cans; however, children primarily use their hands to dig and create endless rivers, damns, hills, and ponds. Water is accessible at a raised basin specifically built for this purpose, with six spigots that can be reached easily by even the youngest child. There are no wheel toys such as tricycles or pathways for such vehicles, but stilts, balls, wooden blocks, tires, and jump ropes are common equipment. Learning to swim during the hot, humid days of spring and summer is part of the curriculum; therefore, there is a small raised swimming pool on the grounds. A vegetable garden changes with every season, and colorful child-created signs indicate what is growing in each of the cultivated rows. Rabbit hutches located in a corner of the yard house the school's pets. This outside space is rich in choices of ways children might play, including messy sand, water, and mud activities.

Children are brought to the lab school, Kyushu Otani Yochien, by buses provided by the school. Because of the different arrival schedules, there is a long period of outside play during arrival time. Therefore, for approximately

An abundance of dirt, sand, and water are available in the Japanese kindergarten play area.

Water is easily accessible for play and cleanup.

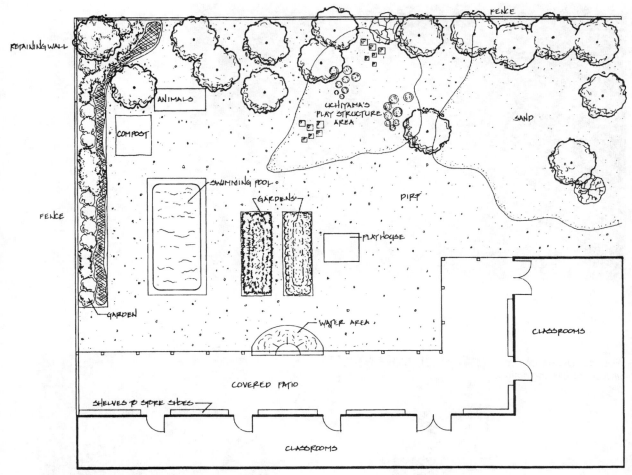

Kyushu Otani Yochien.
Play areas, including building's verandah used for children's activities during rainy weather.

two hours children freely choose among various outside play activities. After all have arrived, the children gather outside with their classes for morning exercises and group play activities. By ten o'clock the children move into their separate classroom areas for more structured lessons. Only 20 minutes a day are spent by the teacher in presenting a particular lesson to the whole group of children. Lunches are brought from home, but everyone is provided tea and morning and afternoon snacks from a central kitchen. Children usually eat outside on a covered porch in their classroom groups with their teacher. At the end of day, the children are again able to play freely outside

A small swimming pool, common at Japanese preschools. A garden with child-created signs and a compost pile are adjacent.

Most Japanese schools have animals; rabbits are common pets.

Children gather with teachers outside before going into their classrooms.

as they wait for the buses to take them home. The days begin and end with these long, unstructured outside play sessions.

I was interested in an unusual play structure designed and built by Professor Uchiyama during the time he served as president of the lab school. It represented his views about the kind of outside experiences he valued for young children. Believing that there must be adequate attention given to their physical development, Uchiyama wanted to create something different from the high, fixed metal structures commonly found on school grounds. He wanted to build something that was beautiful, so he used natural materials. He wanted this structure to convey a special meaning to children, "to speak to them in a way so that they might know nature." Using tree branches, rope, logs, and rocks, he created a climbing place located on a small dirt hill. During construction, Uchiyama talked to the children, explained the building process, the reasons it was being created for them. I watched

Uchiyama's play structure, built of natural materials, is unusual in Japanese school environments.

children use the play area as a lookout, a place for private conversations, a place to chase each other, and an area to develop and demonstrate physical prowess and skills. The physical structure created by Uchiyama is unique, built to represent his belief.

Stepping up from the outside play area is a raised porch, a protected outside multiuse space. All classrooms open onto this covered space which is like a verandah that runs the entire length of the classroom building. Children's shoes are stored on shelves adjacent to their classrooms, making it easy to change to outside or inside shoes. When it rains, many physical activities take place on this porch, such as ball games, using balance beams, and stilt walking. When classroom tables and chairs are moved outside, the verandah is used as an eating area.

Each of the eight classes is housed in a large room with a piano in one corner and tables in the center. When the tables are not in use, they are often stacked and moved to the side to provide a larger open space. I was surprised

Shoes are stored outside, adjacent to classrooms in a long porch area.

that small centers for art, science, reading, or dramatic play, with which I was familiar in the United States, were not a part of the inside classroom environment.

There is a sequence to the day as children in large groups, but without regimentation, move from inside, to porch, to outside activities. Children help teachers set up tables and chairs on the verandah for lunch, and futons inside for naps. As I watched, it seemed that teachers did the work they needed to do, cleaning and organizing, while children helped or played. I realized how different this was from my teaching experiences. I tried to set up my teaching space to reflect what I valued by bringing my own childhood experiences into the day-care environment. There were tree stumps in the hallway for touching, climbing over. We felt, ate, and watched snow melt. Sand and water were available inside in portable containers. This individual classroom personalization by the teacher was not part of the environment I observed in Japan.

I began to understand the impact of my Japanese experiences when, halfway through our two years in Japan, my husband and I took a break and returned to California for a few weeks. As we were driving down the streets of Pasadena, we looked at each other in amazement and asked, "Have they widened the streets since we've been gone?" Upon departing for Japan the previous year, we had felt that Pasadena was crowded and noisy. Twelve months on a small island with millions of people changed our perspective. I began to wonder what other less obvious perspectives were changing. We realized we were learning a great deal about ourselves, our work, and our beliefs by immersing our daily lives in another environment, in another culture.

Design Elements   Many outside school environments in Japan are predictably alike. There is a sameness in design, whether in the rural countryside on the island of Kyushu, in the northern cold climate of the Japanese Alps near Nagano, or in the busy urban areas surrounding Tokyo. Schoolyards have few trees, limited but similar climbing equipment, large open expanses of dirt and sand, an absence of cement, asphalt, and fencing, but accessible water areas. Most schools, no matter what age group they serve, include outside swimming areas and vegetable gardens. School environments for children between infancy and seven years of age seem to focus on the following four elements: an emphasis on nature, opportunities for physical challenge, clarity through consistent markers, and spatial openness.

Nature   The current Japanese Ministry of Education's *Guidelines for Kindergarten Education* (Ishigaki 1989) emphasize the outdoor environment. One of the four major sections of the guidelines advocates "the development of interest in the environment and various phenomena through contact with nature . . . keeping in touch with nature . . . recognition of its beauty and mystery."

> ✦*In my childhood, I played in a park, in a vacant lot, in a hut, wherever my friends and I wanted. I feel now that while I was playing, I learned how to live in Japanese society. I don't see children playing outside as much. . . . I am happy about the new emphasis on the [outside] environment in the day care regulations. I want children to have a chance to play again in many kinds of environments.*
> —Obana 1989, p. 13

Japanese children are asked to understand where they are, in time and place, as a part of the overall cycles of nature—the first snow, the changing colors on trees by the temple, the flowers in the school entryway. Attention to detail is evident in children's artwork. Walks around the community to gather seeds, to notice flowers, or to collect insects are frequent. Even the very young children sketch outdoors, and this continues through the ado-

Searching for insects and flowers reflects the emphasis on the importance of nature.

lescent years when field trips become much more extensive. It is not uncommon to come upon school children huddled together in small groups under umbrellas, in a drizzling rain, sketching the first fragile petals of spring iris that has edged a pond with all the shades of purple.

The outside school yard is dominated by dirt and sand. Asphalt, concrete and grass are uncommon. The water areas are large, centrally located, and easy for children to use, making it possible to create mud or moisten the sand. These mud/sand/water activities occur no matter what the season.

> ◆*In Japan, children usually can play outside with sand and water, however, not in neat sandpits or small water basins because there is plenty of sand everywhere. . . . They can get water themselves in plastic bottles from taps . . . they use everything from jugs and old pans to buckets and tubs. Children find many uses for the sand and water as they "cook", wash, build, or drag sand and water around . . . a real child's paradise!*
>
> —Rijnen 1990, p. 22.[*]

It is believed that nature must be part of the children's daily experience in order for them to recognize its beauty, mystery, and appreciate its changes over time. While principal at Kyushu Otani Yochien, Professor Uchiyama

★ By permission, International Association for the Child's Right to Play (IPA), Jose Rijnen.

Huddled under umbrellas in the rain, children sketch flowers edging the pond.

built a play structure using tree branches and limbs, ropes, rocks, and hills of dirt to represent the natural world in the children's physical life out-of-doors. Vegetable gardens form familiar edges of play spaces. Produce from the garden, such as the sweet potato, marks a particular season, a time of year, and is recognized and celebrated as something that comes around again and again. Activities form around nature's cycles: time to search for bugs in the tall grasses during the warm humid days of early summer, or to gather sheets of ice that seem magically to form with the first freezing nights of fall.

Physical Testing   Children in this country are encouraged to control their bodies. Physical testing is not a demonstration of individual skill proficiency but of group learning through perseverance. Instilling a spirit of perseverance has a long history in Japan (Yamaguchi and Kojima 1979).

> ◆*It is a commonly held belief that the body is greatly malleable as long as the will is strong enough. The terms "gaman suru" (to persevere) and "ganbare" (hold out) are often heard in this context, and have a very positive flavor.*
>
> —Morsbach 1978, p. 7

In relay races, even the youngest participate as part of a team, receiving much encouragement: "Ganbare!" A toddler, lagging behind, only half-way

"Ganbare!" Teachers encourage three-year-olds as they complete their running activity.

around a course, falling and picking himself up again to finally cross the finish line, is warmly embraced and praised for his perseverance. A group of very young children carefully learning to descend a staircase are encouraged by the clapping and chanting of their peers and teachers. There is a great deal of freedom given to young children as a willingness to let them learn to control their own bodies. Even decisions about how much clothing to wear are often left up to the children. Children are frequently seen in all stages of undress. Some wear sweaters and long pants. Others are stripped to the waist with only underpants, even in winter.

The large open dirt areas at schools seem to make sense. Here teams of children run relays, jump over classroom made obstacles of papier mâchée, gather for the early morning "washing" exercises, or participate in folk dancing. Physical activity is important in everyday Japanese life, where workers and students of all ages participate in early morning group exercises. National Sports Day in October is a time when children in schools through-out the country engage in team relays. Families gather on school grounds to celebrate the children's physical learning which is based on being part of a group effort rather than individual competition. No matter what age or what skill level the children have achieved, trying hard, perseverance, is emphasized, not winning.

Six children race as a relay team during National Sports Day events.

Japanese children's learning to control their bodies, taking physical risks, challenges American thinking about safety issues. Teachers' dire warnings of consequences, the constant "Be careful, you'll fall," are not heard in Japan. Children in the United States are seen by Japanese teachers as physically protected. Emiko Ishigaki, dean of the doctoral program in early childhood education at Seiwa College, speaks of the role of the environment as giving children an opportunity to develop physically (Ishigaki 1980). Children, particularly boys, must be encouraged to argue physically among themselves in order to understand how to fit into society as adults. This physical interaction assists their development in both gross motor, and social skills. Roughhousing in preschool seems to be considered a natural part of a child's life, and teachers don't take a "role", other than to simply let it happen. Adults assume that children have physical control over their situations or, if they need an adult, know where to find one.

> ◆At a day care center where there was all sorts of high climbing, rope jumping and stilt walking occurring in patterns that did not translate into my western mind as very safe, I asked if they ever had accidents. Yes, I was told, "occasionally." I then asked if the parents were upset. The answer was emphatic! "Oh, yes, they are always very upset. They apologize to everyone for the trouble that their child caused and often they bring a gift."
>
> —Prescott, personal letter, 1995

Roughhousing, risk taking, and physical conflict are permitted, in part because it is believed in Japan that today's children are not acquiring the necessary socializing ability in the home setting as they did in the past. The current birth rate in Japan is declining and now stands at 1.53 child per family (Okudo 1993). Sibling play is missing. Children get fewer opportunities to play with friends, to experience the fun of group dynamics. They tend to play alone at home with their many toys and video games. Hard working fathers frequently leave early in the morning and arrive home after the child's bedtime. Therefore, many children are growing up with an often-absent father and with few opportunities to play, converse, and share together as a family (Iwata and Hara 1995). Kindergarten programs may be the only places where group play happens. Physical play is believed to be essential in establishing human relationships with others and finding one's place in the group. Therefore, the outside environment must be designed to support these physical activities and social interactions.

Consistent Markers   In the United States we use fences to help people understand limits, areas, edges. Fences are markers that help us understand appropriate behavior and claim particular spaces and serve as a form of control. Outside areas in Japanese schools are large, expansive open spaces with, sometimes, perimeter fencing. During morning exercise activities the very young are in the center of a circle created by the bodies of the older children. Toddlers are safely collected in this space and are able to see the kinds of exercises they will learn as their abilities grow with their size. They are protected, but physically part of the whole group.

Surface changes mark areas and help people understand expected behavior. Sand and dirt play means wearing outside shoes. Decks that join the interior classroom area to the outside play areas are spaces where you leave your messy shoes and change to inside slippers. Decks are not only transition spaces but also places to eat lunch and play areas during rainy weather. Inside, wooden floors surfaces form a contrast with the tatami mats that are frequently a part of the interior environment. These fragrant woven rice straw spaces are more fragile, and inside slippers are not worn on them, children go barefoot instead. Children immediately assume a calm, quiet stance as

During morning exercises, the youngest children are gathered in the center.

Outside porches are places to play during rainy weather.

Tatami mat areas mark quiet places in the school environment.

soon as their feet touch the tatami mat. This straw surface provides a soft place for an afternoon nap or a spot to relax and engage in a quiet activity.

Clothing also marks the environment. Children know their group, without fencing, by the bright colored hats they wear. The purple group, the yellow group, the pink group, the blue group are all extremely visible indicators to children and adults. Even when children choose to wear only underpants, a hat is usually worn, denoting group membership. Backpacks and uniforms indicate age, school, area, and group. Markers are clear and consistent, whether in physical aspects of the built environment or in the clothing that is worn. They are the same in homes and schools, in cities and villages, and throughout the country. Once a person can read these markers, such as bathroom slippers and tatami mats, it is easier to understand the cultural expectations of behavior and the accompanying spatial design elements.

Spatial Openness Japanese cultural values are reflected in the arrangement and use of space. Each preschool class is housed in a room with flexible sparse furnishing. The curriculum activity areas typical of preschools in the United States are usually not seen in Japan. These activity areas for art, dramatic play, blocks, etc., encourage individual and small-group play, which is not a Japanese educational goal. The open space in a Japanese kindergarten fosters large-group interaction and physical play. This arrangement gives Japanese children the everyday experiences necessary to becoming an adult in their culture.

The smaller divisions of space common in preschools in the United States are set up to encourage individual choice. A Japanese graduate student attending a college in Southern California writes about how he felt bombarded with too many choices while living in the United States:

> ◆An American host will ask a guest whether he would like a strong or soft drink, then what kind. . . . He has to give instructions as to how much he wishes to drink, how he wants it served. . . . One has to decide whether one wants it [coffee or tea] with sugar, and milk, and so on. I soon realized this was only the American's way of showing politness to his guest, but in my own mind I had a strong feeling that I couldn't care less. What a lot of choices they were obliging one to make! It seemed to me as if American people valued self-assertion and were convinced of their freedom in each choice.
>
> —Kikuchi 1984, p. 3

What does the arrangement of space teach children about making a choice? Are children sometimes confused, in the same way Michi experienced the confusion of choice making?

Implications

We see environments through a cultural lens which organizes the elements of time and space and the ways in which people interact within them. The cultural lens is born out of generations of ritual and change. Each environment is made up of families and communities with a history. It is difficult to see the impact of culture on the environment in our everyday life. We often live as if we are saying, "Of course, this is how people should live in this environment" (Lakin 1994). We look at outside play yards and say, "Of course, this is the way a school playground should look."

We become clearer about why we arrange environments the way we do by questioning what we believe, by defining the way things "should" be, and looking at cultural opposites to fine-tune our thinking. Revisiting our assumptions about the importance of nature, physical challenge, markers, and open space, in the design of early childhood outdoor environments in Japan, raises questions that impact our assessment of outside educational settings in the United States.

Do the familiar school calendars on each bulletin board decorated with seasonal icons replace a child's direct outdoor experience with the cycles of nature, time, and changing seasons? Learning the months of a year is an exercise in memorization, whereas the seasonal smell of a ripening sweet potato makes physical sense in the lives of children. How do we stimulate all of a child's senses so that the outdoor experience includes new and surprising smells, views, touches, tastes, and sounds? Shouldn't nature simply exist in all its rich diversity outside the classroom door, in a view from the windows, in a walk across the play space? Mud, sand, and water are simple and inexpensive alternatives to asphalt. Inclusion of these elements in a school environment doesn't need to result in maintenance difficulty. Inasmuchas children frequently change into jackets and sweaters to go outside, why not include outside shoes as part of this routine and thus solve problems of tracking mud and sand into interior spaces?

Americans value initiative that is not adult directed. A child's first step, first word, and first drawing are marked as important accomplishments. We know these steps, words, and drawings are self-directed and cannot be forced. On the other hand, we omit clear markers in our school environment that would clarify behavior and, instead, spend time telling children what to do. By directing children with our words, are we setting up patterns of seeking adult approval and thus restrict initiative? Do children depend on adults' spoken cues? Cleanup after a messy mud experience is an easier task for a small person to do on her own when water is available at a strategically placed child-size sink. Closer to the ground than adults, children notice surfaces, but adults seem to forget that spaces and behavior can be described by what is on the ground. The changes from dirt, to cement porch, to wood floor, to tatami mat mark different activities clearly and consistently to the child. Adults are not needed to remind children what to do in each of these spaces. Physical markers can tell us, even as complete strangers, the expected behavior—umbrella stands in every Japanese department store are reminders that you don't carry your umbrella through the area.

We want children to be independent problem solvers, but perhaps we undermine this process by limiting physical challenges in the name of economics, safety, and liability. Has design of outdoor space lost its creative challenges because we are listening to people in power state, "My criteria for a good outdoor area is that the equipment is designed to last 40 years and the insurance company approves the setup" (school administrator, 1995). We value autonomy but limit the ways we let children learn to control their bodies. We value the special potential of each child and strive to support developmental differences, but in the process is the spirit of group cohesiveness lost? Are children developing their potential by choosing tasks beyond their abilities, whereby competition as to who can jump the highest, run the fastest, or throw the farthest dictates what children choose to try to do? Are we designing playgrounds that are limited to competitive physical activities? How can we learn to provide for safety needs while also challenging the physical development of our children? Should group membership and cooperation be considered and/or supported through the physical design of our outside spaces?

The importance of space, whether open or secluded, is different for each of us, depending on our experiences. Open space is essential when gathering as a community is a daily activity. However, even though school children in the United States seldom experience the large-group activities of children in Japan on a regular basis, playgrounds in the United States are often huge expanses of open space. Are we confusing open space with freedom, an important value in this society? Where are the places of refuge for children, the areas outside where a child can find shelter, feel secluded, private? Privacy in Japan is perceived differently. Physical boundaries do not define privacy there in the same way they do in this culture.

Nature, physical challenge, markers, and open space are descriptive dimensions that raise questions and help us see outside environments in new ways. Searching for what is missing provides another view. The physical design of Japanese early childhood programs is congruent with their cultural values. In their sameness, these child-care settings echo the importance of group membership. A visit to several schools in Japan becomes a predictable journey of similarity. One senses the absence of the "particular places," which schools might become through reflections of personal lives, the history of the school, the geography of a region, or the work experiences of families. These schools are not unique; they do not seem to have their own past or particular process of evolution over time.

Japanese early childhood teachers are not shaping their surroundings for themselves. The individual statement of the adult in these settings is difficult to find. Professor Uchiyama's play structure is an interesting exception. Although there is a great deal of flexibility provided by the open space and movable furnishings, adults seem to be trained to fit into the system, which includes the physical environment. They don't change it. They are trained to hold their teaching position for relatively short time periods and to accept the ways adults consistently use both inside and outside space. Every teacher knows how to play the piano, sing the same songs, organize team relays, teach the short directed lessons. Translating personal experiences into the daily routine with children is not what Japanese teachers do.

Privacy, places to be alone, seclusion seem to be missing in Japanese kindergarten environments. Perhaps children are learning at a very early age to find their private spaces within themselves, rather than those defined by a physical boundary. In a crowded country, this may make sense. Where a culture values group membership, it also fits. For an American, however, it can be extremely difficult. Accustomed to depending on physical boundaries, solid walls, doors that close, we can be confused when these barriers are unpredictably penetrated by others. This difference, this missing element of a space to "call my own," emphasized for me the importance of concepts that are not held in common by the two cultures.

What we do hold in common is a conviction that all children need to learn through play. In *Kodomo to Asobi* (1984), author Kouji Kubota writes that children today are unable to play because there are not the places, time, friends, and knowledge of play. He explains that the new Japanese guidelines are a reflection of perceived changes in the family and social life of Japanese children. Educators are asked now to look at planned and unplanned environments as crucial factors in the learning and development of the young child. This is good advice, no matter what our history or cultural perspective.

References

Ishigaki, Emiko H. 1980. "How do we educate teachers for early childhood education." *Bulletin of Seiwa College, 8.*

———. 1989. (Translation.) *New Guidelines for Kindergarten Education: A Summary.* Seiwa College, Japan.

———. 1991. "What is the goal of early childhood care and education?" Unpublished paper. Seiwa College, Japan.

Iwata, Naoko, and Koko Hara. 1995. "Issues of children's play in Japan today." *PlayRights.* 17(3): 30–31.

Kikuchi, Michioki. 1984. *Preschool children in different cultures.* Master's thesis, Pacific Oaks College, Pasadena, CA

Kubota, Kouji. 1984. *Kodomo to Asobi.* Tokyo, Japan: Seibundou-Shinkousha.

Lakin, Mary Beth. 1994. "Observing from a different point of view." *Childcare Information Exchange* 75(January/February): 65–69.

Moore, Robin. 1990. *Childhood's Domain: Play and Place in Child Development.* Berkeley, CA: MIG Communications.

Morsbach, H. 1978. "Socio-psychological aspects of persistence in Japan." *The Japan Times.* December 20, pg. 7.

Obana, Yuji. 1989. *A comparison study of free play time in preschools in Japan and Pasadena.* Masters thesis, Pacific Oaks College, Pasadena, CA.

Okudo, Rikuko. 1993. "Report on IPA activities—Japan." *PlayRights* 15(2): 25–27.

Plath, D. 1980. "Japan, jawpen, and the attractions of an opposite." In *Learning from Shogun: Japanese History and Western Fantasy*, edited by H. Smith. Santa Barbara, CA: University of California Press.

Rijnen, Jose. 1990. "Playing with water in Japan and in the Netherlands." *PlayRights.* 13(3): 22–23.

Shigaki, Irene S. 1983. "Child care practices in Japan and the United States." *Young Children.* (May): 13–24.

Tobin, Joseph J., David Y. H. Wu, and Dana H. Davidson. 1989. *Preschool in Three Cultures; Japan, China and the USA.* New Haven, CN: Yale University Press.

Yamaguchi, Momoo, and Setsuko Kojima, eds. 1979. *A Cultural History of Japan.* Tokyo, Japan: Kenkyusha Printing.

6

$\diamond \diamond$

BACK TO BASICS

INTRODUCTION

I am trying to remember the circumstances that led us to look closely at the role of the outside environment and teacher comfort. When we were observing, it was our custom to meet together over lunch, a time we set aside to shed our objectivity, vent our frustrations, and share playfully the events of the morning. It was here that we puzzled over teachers who had been models of patience indoors, but suddenly turned into irritable army generals barking orders and prohibitions once they set foot outside. We complained too. We complained about the sun beating down on the hot asphalt, about the interminable standing because there was no place to sit or to perch. We grumbled about the playhouses and climbing structures that blocked our view just as the child we were watching sprinted across the yard to begin a new activity.

We also marveled! There was the elderly teacher in charge of far too many two-year-olds who carried her aluminum folding chair into the very ordinary play yard and sat down, right in the middle of everything. Children climbed onto her lap, nestled in her arms as she called out encouragement and compliments for things well done to the active players. And there was the young, obviously inexperienced teacher who had real troubles in the classroom, but outdoor sat calmly on a shady platform adjoining the climber as the children set about genuinely creative play.

Once it dawned on us that there was a relationship between the puzzle over the transmogrified teachers, complaints about our own discomforts, and the marvels about why some seeming inept teachers look so competent once they move from indoors to outdoors. It was the physical space! Sometimes it supported the adult and sometimes it didn't. Why had it taken so long for us to see it? I think that the answer lay in our naiveté. We assumed that if a space looked attractive to our adult eyes it must be a good space, and vice versa. Of course, some spaces are both unattractive and nonfunctional, but it was not until we had done much more observing and thinking that we began to hammer out some principles for talking about why spaces work.

—ELIZABETH PRESCOTT

Life is experienced as more satisfying and interesting, and is therefore more meaningful and conducive to growth when space invites us to do what we want to do.

— Kritchevsky and Prescott 1969, p. 5

W hat is often lost in the analysis of educational settings is how the spaces also support adults who spend a major portion of their working day there. Adults have needs and preferences that may not relate to the children's activities; however, the physical environment rarely reflects this. Teachers are seldom asked to describe their favorite outdoor places or to imagine creating an environment based on what they might need during their working day. Suffering tiny chairs, aching feet, and sun squinted eyes is simply accepted as the way it is. Adults in children's environments don't think about the space as something they can share—after all, it's for the children. Designers, therefore, focus site analysis on children's activities and fail to consider spaces that might invite adults to do what they need to do. The nine pairs of elements presented in Chapter 2 take a different form when there is focus on the adult point of view. Teacher preferences—watching, resting, and socializing—are discussed in detail in this chapter as we go back to basics and apply those design guidelines to the adults who share outside play spaces.

To understand why outdoor educational environments tend to take forms that lack consideration of adult needs, it is helpful to look at the factors that affect school design decisions. First, we let stereotypical expectations and traditional views of "women's" work influence the way we think about adult activities in educational settings. Second, congruence, as described in Chapter 4, means a fit between the philosophy or vision of the educator and the children's learning, not necessarily adults' needs. Finally, educational environments are usually simplified and have a "look-alike" appearance as the result of segregation of children by age, sameness of materials, and routinization of tasks.

Reflections of "Women's Work"

✦*Although beautification of dwellings preocccupies many a homemaker, comparable consideration is rarely given to child-care spaces. These settings, by virtue of their anonymous ownership . . . become an aesthetic no-man's-land designed more to assist the custodian who maintains them than the users who must grow within them.*

—Olds 1987, p. 137

Teaching as a profession has traditionally been dominated by females, and, therefore, stereotypical limitations of gender roles narrow our view. The organization of living environments—rooms to sleep in, areas in which to gather and share food, spaces used to take care of personal needs, this interior arranging that women do in homes— spills over into the school setting. Women's work at home has been viewed traditionally as keeping the house clean, being in charge of how it is decorated, and doing most of the arranging of furnishings. Keeping the interior school environment orderly, clean, and pleasingly decorated is also viewed as the teacher's responsibility (Loughlin and Suina 1982).

Even though teachers are active in setting up their interior classroom spaces, the area outside the classroom door is usually viewed as someone else's territory. In home gardens, women may add color and texture or enjoy planting annual flower beds, but men usually engage in the "heavier" maintenance work—lawn mowing, tree pruning, irrigation system repair. The outside school grounds are also mowed, pruned, repaired, irrigated, and overseen by male staff. Selection and placement of trees, shrubs, and flowers are maintenance rather than educational decisions. Teachers accept these role definitions. When children are outside, they are no longer in a tradition-ally viewed "female" space. These limitations to our view of male and female activities in home environments seem to influence our expectations of adult behavior in educational settings. The interior spaces receive the educator's attention, rather than the outside play areas. Sweeping, decorating, picking up, organizing, and cleaning off dominate the involvement with physical space. It fits traditional role expectations.

Although our views of male and female roles are changing, the activities in a home setting continue to influence our expectations of teacher behavior in relation to safety as well as maintenance. Traditionally, women are still seen as those who comfort the tears and bandage the toddler's skinned knee, who worry more about a potential tricycle spill, who provide careful reminders about safely crossing the street.

Ensuring children's safety and security during their daily play has been the territory of females, particularly in the past when males were usually working during the day and unable to perform these tasks. Making sure children are safe at all times in a world that has become increasingly unsafe is a major issue for teachers. Surveillance for potential hazards eclipses observation of children's recreational activities in the playground. Teachers do spend time watching the children, but safety issues dominate the views.

A safe and well-maintained outside environment is important in any children's setting. It is to be expected that designers focus their assessment of adult user needs on maintenance and security. After all, teachers no doubt emphasize these problems when working with a designer. The resulting design solution including fencing, asphalt, and storage sheds is predictable. The lack of richness and diversity in the outside space is, unfortunately, understandable. Teachers add flexible elements to enrich the child's play space, but seldom is the environment analyzed as to how adult experiences might be enriched.

Reflections of Teacher's Philosophy

✦*Schools are not created to foster the intellectual and professional growth of teachers. The assumption that teachers can create and maintain those conditions which make school learning and school living stimulating for children, without those same conditions existing for teachers, has no warrant in the history of man.*
—Sarason S. 1971, pp. 123–124.

Rather than addressing adults' needs, the typical school environment reflects the adults' beliefs about how education for children should take place. Teachers approach children's activities with vastly varied philosophies and different thresholds of comfort for living with the consequences of children's play. A place to experience mud may be a delight for one teacher, recapturing memories of childhood. For another, this activity simply means cleanup problem. A pond filled with pollywogs and plants may be integral to the curriculum plans of one teacher, highlighting a science program. But another teacher may see the space only as a safety problem. Outside environments that invite children to engage in activities that fit the philosophy and goals of the teacher are congruent, but are they also stimulating for adults? What might adults need to be invited to do in the space? The concept of outdoor play environment as a place that must meet the needs of adults has not received much attention (Prescott 1987).

Reflections of Sameness

We segregate the infant, the preschooler, the school-age child, the teenager into their own bounded areas. Child care settings further separate the babies from the toddlers, the threes from the fours. These chronological age groupings help to simplify a teaching curriculum geared to meeting the growth and development needs of children. Although there is a wide range of individual differences in any group of children, most educational programs see some value in clustering children with others of the same age, assuming curriculum can be fashioned in a developmentally age-appropriate way.

The environment is further simplified and limited by the types of materials used to build outside settings and by the available furnishings. Chain link fences, asphalt or concrete bike pathways, metal storage sheds, sand beneath swings, and small tables with benches or child sized chairs, usually plastic with metal legs, are all familiar in outside educational settings. It is difficult for teachers to experience a range of complexity, or a richness of texture and diversity of view when the outside environment is so simplified. The aspect of a metal slide with black rubber matting below is not a multisensory experience for the adult in charge. Spending portions of every day in a setting where the view is enclosed by metal fencing and dominated by hard surfaces offers little change in color, texture, or form. It becomes a setting of sameness, both in form and activity. How different is the adult outside experience at a beachside strand where all ages mingle, their differences offering a sensory feast! The spirited pre-teenager charges past the white-haired couple playing chess. The smell of hot dogs and French fries fills the air. Activities vary from fishing to roller blading, while the distant view of quiet, white tipped waves moving endlessly toward a sandy beach seems to change continually. In contrast, the school environment is a reflection of sameness. No wonder it is easy for adults who work in children's settings to become routinized and bored over time (Prescott and Jones 1972)

Adding to the routinization of tasks owing to the lack of variety in the outdoor physical setting is the fact that expectations of adult behavior involving the organization, arrangement, or provisioning of the outside space are also limited and simplified. When cleaning and watching dominate adult activities in an outside area, the opportunities to experience personal challenge and moments of joy are severely curtailed. Boredom is increased. Although the child may find many adult-provided activities to choose from on that fenced asphalt, teachers are left with a hard, simple, and permanent space that they stand in and survey.

On the other hand, the out-of-doors may offer the adult a potential freedom, because things outside are not limited by their inherent intentionality. Unlike classroom interiors, outside areas have few manufactured furnishings that are associated with a particular use. Inside the classroom, a desk dictates certain activities. You don't dance on it or sit under it, you work at your desk. The chalkboard means *stand, write on and use to teach others who are watching what you are writing.* Shelves mean *keep things in order, store, organize.* Bulletin boards are decorated, changed from time to time, display a certain pattern of quality. The rug is to sit on, stand on or to gather on. Behaviors inside are limited and defined by these traditional classroom forms. But outside, the benches, sand, dirt, and trees don't limit and define behaviors. Unlike a desk inside, a bench outdoors can become a place to share with others, a platform to pile pillows on, a place to stand on to reach a high flowering branch, a retreat that can be moved into the shade of a tree, a spot to eat lunch, or an edge that holds planter boxes offering a cascade of spring scents and color.

Although an outside area is freeing because of its lack of furnishings that define particular behaviors, it can also be very difficult for the adult to know what to do outside. Without rugs, chairs, desks, or walls, the task is like arranging spaces without rooms, setting up areas with no furnishings. How are outside spaces defined, made different from each other, and designated as unique places where a variety of contrasting activities can take place? Without a desk to work at, a chalkboard to write on, a rug to gather on, supplies to organize, what is the adult's role outside? How can the outside space support adult choices beyond surveillance and maintenance?

There is only limited opportunity for adults to use and change an outside environment if it is defined by only surface (grass, asphalt, cement) differences. Outside spaces that are boring for children will also be boring for adults. Yet the environment could be like a busy sidewalk cafe, offering endless interesting things to watch and conversations on which to eavesdrop.

Adult Needs

◆*A productive teaching/learning environment is one in which both teachers and children can thrive. An environment in which an individual can thrive is one which offers him or her the maximum number and variety of choices with which he or she can cope at a given time.*
—Jones 1978, p. 43

Outside spaces that are freeing to adults invite them to choose their activity based on their needs. "Complexity [for children] is viewed as the potential that the setting and its props offer for manipulation and alteration" (Prescott 1987, p. 76). For adults, complexity is the potential to be active in changing something, to solve problems, to test ideas and the philosophy of teaching in action. It is a process of developing congruence over time.

What are the elements in the outdoor environment that adults value? What kinds of spaces do they avoid? What are adults naturally attracted to outside? What do adults like or dislike outside in play areas and why? What is basic for the adult who works with children? To answer these questions, adults who work in day-care facilities, elementary and high school settings, and children's museums were asked to identify in their workplaces their favorite and least favorite outside areas. They were questioned about what they need during their long, busy days. Even though these educators work in very different settings, the similarity of response was surprising. They described searching for spaces that support three different types of adult activities: (1) watching children initiate their own complex play activities, (2) rest, retreat, and relaxation, and (3) socializing with adults and making connections to the larger community in which they work.

The nine dimensions presented in Chapter 2, seen from the child's point of view, are now revisited in relation to the adult users who share children's outside areas. The traditional tasks of maintaining and securing the play space are not discarded; however they no longer limit our understanding of adult outside activities. Instead, teachers' descriptions of what they *enjoy* doing guides the selection of basic design elements. Using observation, relaxation, and connecting to the community as desired adult activities, the nine pairs of elements are reconsidered to discover ways to shape outside play space that supports these valued activities. This approach can guide the process of creating a better match between people and place.

Observation   Teachers described the pleasure they experienced sitting on the sidelines of child-initiated activities, watching children freely play and explore. Observing interesting things with water and sand or dirt held great fascination for them. They mentioned the joy they felt when a child was able to make a bubble as large as his own body. Eavesdropping on children's conversations is a part of observation that teachers value. Listening-in is especially interesting when children try to solve problems, such as how they might build a fort that would work even if it rained. By watching the spontaneous play of children, adults reconnect with the meaning of their work:

> *The huge sand area, with lots of water. . . . watching kids was wonderful, it was an unbelievable place.*

> *When I feel bored to death, hating something, I watch; it's really special to see the kids explore, I know this is why I do this work.*

Seating for adults in children's play areas is often physically uncomfortable.

Loved to watch the kids dressed up, the dramatic play; it was magical, I felt like a child just watching them.

It was a special moment for me, overhearing her say "Oh, that water won't go this way," as she tried and tried to use the hose to create a small stream that went uphill to the bridge.

Relaxation Places with just enough privacy, retreat spots to meet personal relaxation needs, were valued spaces. These places, usually away from children where an adult could go for a much needed break, were fondly mentioned as "hideaways" or "like my little cave" or "my log." The descriptions of adult retreat areas always include natural elements such as grass, trees, bushes, or "veggies and flowers." The places might be valued because of the intimate scale of the immediate surroundings, such as bark, pebbles, or seed pods, or because of a distant view, a flowering tree, a rocky hillside or a cloud-filled sky. Teachers mentioned wanting to be in touch with the season or the changing weather patterns. They valued animals in the environment—both natural, such as squirrels scrambling up tree trunks, or as part of a program, like rabbits and ducks. Animals in an outdoor setting added to that closer-to-nature feeling for the adults.

Mulberry trees are magical—
cool, shady, safe, contained—
a lush jungle in harmony with nature, with natural colors,

The yard was quiet and peaceful in that special corner,
a wonderful combination of grass, trees, and sky.

That tree, I can also see it out my window; I get a feeling
of well being by sharing a space with nature.

I love to go to the butterfly garden, the earth works,
the natural parts of our place.

There is a log, behind a tree, I could just sit there and really notice the bark, the acorns, the tiny green growth—feel close to nature and then feel relaxed.

A special corner place on a school yard, among natural elements, provides some sense of retreat for a teacher.

In contrast, places "disliked" by adults are dusty and exposed. Teachers frequently mentioned trees that were missing, leaving a barren and hot area now avoided. They described places that seemed "dead" and boring because plants no longer grew there. Contrasts were made between the negative qualities of open, exposed areas and the positive qualities of the perimeters of outside environments that seemed to provide some sense of enclosure. Exposed play areas are avoided when adults seek seclusion and sense of place for themselves.

> *Full of junk, everything depressing, ratty looking—impossible place, so dirty and dusty.*
>
> *Couldn't see good stuff due to dirt and mess.*
>
> *Hard, hot, concrete too open.*

Adults enjoy the secluded edges of a play space. They mentioned "getaway" places for adults, spaces where children are not allowed. These might include the top of a play structure in the early morning before children arrive, or a place between buildings that is off limits for children.

> *Here was intimacy and privacy, a chance in this back space to have quiet conversations with another teacher.*
>
> *Loved the edges, the in-between places that no one knew about.*
>
> *There is a special corner, it feels intimate, my place.*
>
> *Sometimes before the kids arrived I'd sit on the top of the play structure and paint with watercolors, it was a beautiful way to start my day.*
>
> *There used to be a hedge out in front, by the tree. I could sit there and no one knew I was there, private, quiet, green, relaxing; sometimes I'd drink tea there.*

At times these secluded edges were described as perching places—places where adults were away from the rough and tumble of the children, but were still connected. They were, as in the title of an A. A. Milne poem, "half way down the stairs," places where adults could think new thoughts, pause, and sigh.

These halfway points, pausing places, provide space so that "funny thoughts running round my head" might happen to break the sameness of the day, a moment where a person can feel free from the pressures of those defined places waiting beyond.

Community Connections   Alexander (1977, p. 169) describes the importance of finding ways to design places where people see each other and "confirm their community." In public life, plazas, paseos, and town squares are often such places. To feel part of a community, a connection to the whole, where kids and adults mingle naturally is also important in educational settings. Working with children, especially those under five years of age, can be an isolating experience for adults. The need for clear barriers to provide security and safety for children of this age thwarts the adult needs to socialize with peers and maintain connections beyond the sameness of a young child's daily routine. Semiprivate front porches facilitate views of other group activities and the opportunity to observe. Teachers mentioned how they enjoy being in places that provide a connection to something beyond their own program responsibility.

> *Shady Lane was inviting because of the social interaction, liked to just walk down it and look at everything and chat with folks.*

> *The front porch was wonderful, benches, activities, a place where kids and adults mingled naturally, a place to watch, look out on the activity in the yards.*

> *I could look down the lane, see banners, see people, see into other yards, stop by the fence to chat, it's what connected all the yards, all of us.*

A shared circulation area offers a way for adults to connect to the school's community.

Issues of security, which result in fencing, work against adult needs to socialize. Issues of surveillance, which require unobstructed views in all directions, work against adult needs for privacy. The designer faces an important challenge in the planning of outside educational environments for adults who enjoy watching, but also seek privacy, and yet need to maintain connections to the larger community.

> ✦*A teacher who is not learning at least as much as his/her students is bound to get stale. It is not enough to do things because they're "good for the children." Things done should include elements of personal challenge for the teacher, and moments of joy.*
> —Jones and Prescott 1978, p. 38

Learning   Boredom is a problem that can be solved. It is helpful for adults to challenge children to make choices, giving them practice in solving their own feelings of boredom. Unfortunately, we often rush in to let children know what to do, organizing their day with structured activities such as Little League, karate lessons, or video games, and thus deprive them of finding their own solutions. Adults also need to figure out their own problems of boredom, particularly when the environment no longer provides them with challenges. When the daily structure simply means sameness, when the only differences are children's arguments over a piece of equipment or about whether it is cold enough to wear a jacket, teachers are not making interesting choices and ultimately, not thriving.

How does the design of an outside play setting support or hinder adult abilities to learn? How does the sameness that dulls our minds retreat in the face of spicy challenges? Teachers' descriptions of activities they value indicate their need for personal challenge and moments of joy. If the environment is complex, it offers adults opportunities to thrive by making choices. When the environment that supports adult learning is active, flexible, and public, adults get feedback from their actions. Changing a space, acting on it, moving things around, finding out how those changes work are actions that challenge thinking. For example, a community patio may be used as an outdoor market where teachers and/or children sell their own handmade art and crafts, foods prepared at home, and products from the school garden. The outside car barn (shed) at Midland school provides a place for faculty to work with teenagers repairing the various antique vehicles and farm equipment. A wide connecting pathway like Shady Lane at times became a place to hold a car wash, where many join in the fun with bubbles and hose play. A front porch can be transformed into a small stage where a community enjoys the sounds of music and dancing to celebrate a special day in the culture of its citizens. This activity might become a regular event, a communitywide "sing" that marks a shared passage of time for everyone, young and old. In each of these examples, the outside area is flexible enough to support a variety of complex activities initiated by teachers but shared by the community.

> ✦*Good settings respect adults' abilities to learn and adults' needs for comfort.*
>
> —Greenman 1988, p. 6

Comfort   The traditional outside setting of asphalt, cement. chain link fencing, grass field, and play equipment in sand, when analyzed according to the nine elements presented in Chapter 2, is primarily hard, public, people-made, and active. The essential comfort dimensions for adults are missing. Softness for the child may be found in sand, water, and mud, and although adults may enjoy watching the children experience this messy softness, they too need to experience touching the world in a softer way. Natural elements such as flowers and grass can provide a less messy adult softness outside.

As suggested in Whyte's (1980) study of public spaces, adult seating is an important feature even when the outside area is designed primarily for children.

Teachers need a choice of places to sit outside to meet their personal comfort needs.

✦*Choice should be built into the basic design . . . making ledges so they are sittable . . . maximizing the sittability of inherent features.*
—Whyte 1980, p. 28

For adults working with children outside it is important that there be a variety of places where they might choose to sit. These can be built into the inherent features of the space or provided by furnishings. This feature implies flexibility, things that can be moved, but such furnishings are often at the child's scale and not comfortable for the adult. Large logs forming the edges of sand areas or grouped around a tree, raised decks, and retaining walls all potentially provide comfortable, permanent adult seating.

Teachers may enjoy watching children create a secluded place under a sheet or in a cardboard box, but adults need more tangible forms than cardboard and cloth to provide privacy outside. Adult privacy in educational settings is limited to interior architectural forms, in particular, the bathroom and teachers' lounge. These spaces seldom include natural soft elements. Places for adult retreat and relaxation outside that offer views of nature can alleviate exhaustion and "burn out," frequent complaints in child care. When adult needs for comfort are missing, the quality of a person's daily experience is severely limited.

When the day ends and the adult finds him- or herself exhausted, thinking back over the various elements that dominated that particular day, it is often possible to isolate what was missing as softness, nature,

Natural areas are valued by adults who work in child-care settings.

privacy. Adults delay experiencing these elements until weekends or vacations, when they head to the mountains, beaches, lakes, and streams. We seek natural settings—towering trees, open space, uncluttered by concrete. The abundance of water and sand at a beach provide nourishment through softness. Privacy can be achieved in sitting by an isolated river, listening only to the water's journey over smooth stones. These getaway vacations are important, but it also makes sense to rearrange educational settings so an adult needs for privacy and softness can be met on a more regular basis.

A safe, maintained outside space for adults and children who spend time together should be basic to any design. However, using only these two elements as design guides limits what adults are able to do. Choice is missing, and it becomes difficult for adults to move between a variety of spaces in order to meet their different needs. They are trapped in one kind of environment, as one might be on an airplane journey. Confined by a seatbelt, the view is determined and activities limited. Outside educational environments must offer adults more than the endurance test of an airplane flight. Using an adult perspective, it is possible to shape outside play space in more complex ways, offering a choice of activity. Maximum exposure to others—a more public setting that facilitates connections to the community—is one end of a continuum. Somewhere in the middle are those in-between places, the secluded edges, where people are able to perch and watch. Finally, there are the soft natural areas that provide retreat from the endless expenditure of youthful energy. Analyzing an outside space in this way helps to clarify a design process where adult activity becomes a focus of what is basic. By focusing on adults' activities, their preferences and needs, outside play space design expands beyond the limitations of simply maintenance and surveillance issues. A rich vista of possibilities is offered by the different design characteristics that might be used in viewing a setting for children through this adult lens.

Public Spaces— Accessible, Open, Public, Active

✦*Public areas also enable people to connect with others, to affiliate in some way with other people. This may occur in a very passive mode, as in cases where people position themselves to watch the passing scene . . . in other cases a more active participation is desired.*
—Carr et al. 1992, p. 91

Public spaces emphasize exchange. The marketplaces in our historical past are powerful images of areas where commerce, socializing, and learning took place. Plaza areas and town squares are still settings where we learn about others, where we enjoy watching, where we choose to make connections. For 20 years a pancake breakfast on the Fourth of July still attracts thousands because, as one resident noted, "You see everyone you know, and you hang out. I don't think it's so much for the meal. You come to see the townies . . . my doctor . . . Mr. Kahn of Kahn's Shoe Store—my dad taught all his kids" (*The New Mexican*, 5 July, 1995). Public spaces are open and active. To facilitate community connections in school settings, it is important that we plan some part of the outside area using the design elements *accessible, active, open,* and *public* as guides.

Shady Lane at Pacific Oaks, with the comings and goings of people, is similar to a busy town square, a mosaic of changing colorful activities. It is a place where teachers as well as children engage in a variety of activities, which include selling things and sharing a community lunch. It is a place that has endured for more than 60 years as a flexible artery that joins all of the various programs. It is an active connection to the place where people work together, sharing a common philosophy while striving toward similar goals.

Porches provide settings where teachers can observe the larger picture and connect to the daily ebb and flow. At Midland the front porch on Main House is described as a place to enjoy the distant views of Grass

A school's porches provide places to connect with the daily ebb and flow of young people and their activities.

Mountain or of the adjacent barn—a reminder of the school's early beginnings—or watch a passing group of teenagers, fresh from sports, rushing to shower before dinner. Its a place where a person can call out to discover who won the soccer game or ask questions about homework assignments due in the morning. From this porch the mail delivery is visible—another connection. To understand Midland's daily routine, a visitor simply has to spend time on the front porch, listening and watching.

Perching Places— Accessible, Public, Passive

◆*The process of lingering is a gradual one; it happens; people do not make up their minds to stay; they stay or go, according to a process of gradual involvement. . . . The goal-oriented activity of coming and going then has a chance to turn gradually into something more relaxed.*
—Alexander, Ishikawa, and Silverstein 1977, p. 600

Like that point "halfway down the stairs," the secluded edges of play spaces are accessible visually. There people can see and be seen. The views from these edges are out and around, up and down. A connection is maintained on the edges of a place. A person might pause here but privacy by not being

A teacher is able to perch in the background at the secluded edge of this play space.

seen is missing. In this way there is a feeling of connection to what is in view. However, unlike in a public square with its ongoing activity, these places in between are passive places, sitting, contemplating spaces, allowing a moment to stop and make time for thoughts to roam and dance.

Private Spaces—Inaccessible, Private, Passive, Soft, and Natural

◆*The capacity to direct one's attention is a fragile resource. It is worn down by distraction, confusion, and other hassles of various kinds... But perhaps the quintessential micro restorative environment, the one that most closely brings together the multiple themes . . . into a single, small, intensely meaningful space, is the garden.*
—Kaplan and Kaplan 1993, p. 242

Places that nourish us and provide renewal through retreat have similar properties to those of the restorative garden. Such spaces can play an important role in healing the damage caused by the multiple pressures and demands of daily life (Kaplan and Kaplan 1993). For those who work with children and their families on a day-to-day basis, these pressures are immediate, demanding, and seemingly endless. Nature offers a source of rejuvenation; however, natural settings that are restorative and healing are seldom used or valued for such purposes (Olds 1989). We spend the greater part of our days inside buildings that are predictably controlled, where windows seldom open or offer the occupants a vista of earth and sky. It is difficult to retreat even in our imagination to something softer and more natural.

In using retreat as a design element, it is important that outside educational environments have places that are passive, soft, natural, permanent, and private. Nature is seen as providing that soft intimate scale. Teachers at the Armenian school clearly expressed this longing when they sought an outside space with a tree, flowers, or grass. Midland School faculty were accustomed to meet to share coffee under a tree. Even after their "coffee tree" died, the stump remained the center of faculty gatherings during their morning break. The old lemon tree at Sonshine Preschool was a valued reminder of the orchards that once grew on the land. Along with pussy willow, teachers planted vines and shrubs along the chain link fencing as a first step in building a play space. Rejuvenation of the art studio at Pacific Oaks meant that plants were again growing—flowers cascading over the fence, a volunteer tree sprouting where ashes once dominated the area.

The Neighborhood as a Model

Adults look for outside areas that function like a neighborhood with public, semiprivate, and private spaces. Spaces around buildings offer front yard and backyard potential (Cooper Marcus and Wischeman 1978). Public space, especially pathways, provide a chance to make connections to the outside neighborhood. The outside area as a place where people "live" is similar to a neighborhood of families where children and adults share space. Using the neighborhood as a model, perhaps a complex space can be designed where many generations live together, a place where security, surveillance, privacy, and opportunities to socialize are all possible and facilitated by the overall design.

Both Pacific Oaks and Midland function in this way. The pathways between buildings developed over many years of people moving through the space, between front yards, backyards, porches, and other pathways. These are settings that meet adult comfort needs, where privacy isn't limited to a small locked bathroom stall or a vinyl couch in a teacher's lounge. The natural texture of trees, sounds of birds, and scents of grass provide seclusion, the needed "lounge" to renew oneself. These settings have potential for adults to create congruence for themselves in process. These are outdoor areas where at times there is an adult mess: the car barn—a yard overflowing with parts of a process; the art studio—a retreat of calm, contemplative creativity. These are places where you know something about the children who play in them because of the mud and sand, boxes and boards, but you also know something about the adults who spend time there because special places invite and fit big folks. These are outdoor designs that invite people of all ages, sizes, and styles to shape the space to fit who they are and what they need, and then to move on refreshed and intellectually renewed.

References

Alexander, Christopher, S. Ishikawa, and M. Silverstein. 1977. *A Pattern Language.* New York: Oxford University Press.

Carr, S., Mark Francis, Leeanne Rivlin, and Andrew Stone. 1992. *Public Space.* New York: Cambridge University Press.

Cooper Marcus, Clare, and Trudy Wischemann. 1987. "Outdoor spaces for living and learning." *Landscape Architecture.* (March-April) p: 54–61.

Greenman, James. 1988. *Caring Spaces, Learning Places: Children's Environments That Work.* Redmond, WA: Exchange Press.

Jones, Elizabeth, ed. 1978. *Joys and Risks in Teaching Young Children.* Pasadena, CA: Pacific Oaks College.

Jones, Elizabeth, and Elizabeth Prescott. 1978. *Dimensions of Teaching Learning Environments. II, Focus on Day Care* Pasadena, CA: Pacific Oaks College.

Kaplan, Rachel, and Stephen Kaplan. 1993. "Restorative experience: The healing power of nearby nature." In *The Meaning of Gardens*, edited by M. Francis and R. Hester. Cambridge MA: The MIT Press.

Kritchevsky, Sybil, and Elizabeth Prescott. 1969. *Planning Environments for Young Children: Physical Space*. Washington DC: National Association for the Education of Young Children.

Loughlin, Catherine, and Joseph Suina. 1982. *The Learning Environment*. New York: Teachers College Press.

Milne, A. A. 1973. *When We Were Very Young*. New York: Penguin.

Olds, Anita Rui. 1987. "Designing settings for infants and toddlers." In *Spaces for Children: The Built Environment and Child Development*, edited by C. Weinstein and T. David. New York: Plenum Press.

Olds, Anita Rui. 1989. "Nature as healer." *Children's Environments Quarterly* 6(1): 27–32.

Prescott, Elizabeth. 1987. "The environment as an organizer of intent in child-care settings." In *Spaces for Children: The Built Environment and Child Development*, edited by C. Weinstein and T. David. New York: Plenum Press.

Prescott, Elizabeth, and Elizabeth Jones. 1972. *Day Care as a Child-Rearing Environment*. Vol. 2. Washington DC: National Association for the Education of Young Children.

Sarason, Seymour. 1971. *The Culture of the School and the Problem of Change*. Boston, MA: Allyn and Bacon.

Whyte, William. 1980. *The Social Life of Small Urban Spaces*. Washington DC: The Conservation Foundation.

7

✧ ✧

ODE TO THE OUTDOORS

INTRODUCTION

What I remember about my elementary school is the patio. It was actually the size of a large courtyard, but we called it the patio. Its surface was faced green concrete, and a graceful series of arches enclosed it on three side. Though I'm sure I learned a great deal in the classrooms that were located in two-story rows on the long sides of the patio, I have no memory of them—except that most of their windows looked out on the patio.

When I think of my high school, I remember the bayou that ran by it. Dense tangles of trees and undergrowth lined the bayou and made it difficult to get close enough to see the water, which we were forbidden to do. We did anyway, of course, but not often because the bayou was mysterious and a bit frightening. The water was muddy brown and said to be full of alligator gars. As with the elementary school, I remember little of the high school classrooms, though I do recall a large, high-ceilinged entry and gathering space, which was called the rotunda.

I suspect these memories are not much different from those of most others who grew up in mid-century American suburbs. What is interesting about them to me is that it is not the rooms where most learning is commonly believed to occur that I recall, but the small fragments of urban landscape that were left over among the buildings. And I think, too, that these places did much to determine what I would do with my life.

—JOHN LYLE

As childhood has become more restricted, opportunities for interaction with nature and natural experience are even more critical.

—Francis 1995, p. 188

As the cursor moves across the screen, David chooses what to play in his electronic "Back Yard." His companion, Pepper—a friendly voice, encourages choices: "If you want to dig, press the dig button." David clicks on a tractor that chug chugs across the sandbox, which transforms into a treasure hunt. David chuckles as he causes a ball to bounce across the yard into the inflatable pool, with all of the sound effects. This backyard is a two-dimensional image of a tree house, fence, picnic tables, water spigot, and garden. These areas invite exploration as they transform, make sounds, and move when chosen. Although the computer activity is an amusing game, for some children an outside place to play, their range of potential exploration, is rapidly shrinking to the size of an electronic screen. Activities are clicked on; playmates are friendly sounding Peppers. Exploration of this backyard is

A drawing of a computer screen expresses a favorite play activity.

confined to sitting, looking, and choosing within the possibilities of the particular computer program. Discovery is a message, a sound, an image, or a voice saying, *If you want to do something, click, or move the arrow.*

Outdoor Habitats Remembered

Backyards

As I remember my childhood, I recall that my brother spent many hours in our backyard near his favorite tree. I used to tease him when I'd catch him talking to himself as he sat under those bending, protective branches. Children growing up today are fortunate to have access to backyards that provide a safe refuge. Pressures to build to the edges of a lot line, to grow homes on lands that once produced food or provided habitat for critters, are threatening that backyard tree. It is increasingly difficult for children to find spaces outside where it is possible to hide among tree branches and whisper their fears or frustrations.

Backyards and gardens adjacent to a child's home setting evoke strong images, memories we carry with us that influence our attitudes toward outside environments (Francis 1995). According to Francis (p. 184) "Many unstructured or wild areas have been systematically removed from suburban and urban places, including home gardens." It is empowering for a child, to be able to go out a back door into a space where grown-ups are not telling you what to do, to wander into a place of living things that invite you to be an active builder, an explorer, an experimenter. These outside-the-home opportunities have disappeared for many children.

Blocks and Lots

When I was seven years old, and very angry with my mother, I filled a Thermos with water, took a favorite stuffed toy, and announced I was running away from our home, a small duplex in the downtown area of a large southern California city. I remember my feeling of independence, the sense of adventure when I walked all the way around our small neighborhood block. Neighbors knew me; I stopped en route to sip my water, sitting on friendly front lawns. Finally, returning home, by then forgetting what had angered me, I was ready to reenter my world of family membership. Children growing up today are fortunate if they can find those outside escape places, safe because neighbors know and care about the children who live on their block.

Setting up a lemonade stand during the hot, long days of summer, waiting with fist-clutched coins for the sound of the bell on the ice cream truck, selling hand-painted rocks to neighbors—those childhood commercial activities provided important opportunities for social contact. During the summer polio epidemics in the 1940s, children were often encouraged stay indoors or safely away from crowds to avoid contact with this feared contagious disease. Today the epidemic of death by gunshot in children is 10 times greater than those polio epidemics of 50 years ago (Christoffel 1995). Children are being kept from outdoor people-connecting activities once again. The threat and statistics are real and of growing concern. Neighborhood environments that are dominated by threats to a child's physical safety significantly reduce opportunities for contacts with other people and impact social and motor development (Huttenmoser 1995).

Barns and Woods Children today find their access to a range of outdoor places beyond the home setting constrained and controlled by adults. Barnyards filled with the stuff of animal life were once common near family living areas. Wooded ravines and other wild places were often found near homes and neighborhoods. Children could walk to a barn and feed saved carrot tops to familiar horses, ride bikes to a nearby gully and build forts and hideouts with their friends. As our urban settlements increase in size, scope, and scale, farms and forests are pushed farther away, beyond our children's range. A bicycle is seldom able to link a child with barns or woods. Miles of highways have replaced pedestrian pathways that once connected the farm or forest to a child's home base. Now it takes transportation, time, and financial resources for a child to touch the soft velvety nose of a horse or to toss rocks into a creek.

Each year when I ask my design students to describe the ways they remember playing, the places they recall with great fondness, fewer of them recount stories of wild, unkempt areas where they built forts or played in streams. Some tell of growing up in other lands and cultures, where fields edged by irrigation ditches, or tropical fruit trees, or adjacent home gardens fed families and provided places to play. These are in stark contrast to students' descriptions of growing up in urban areas bounded by family fears of traffic, crime, and unsafe places. Many spent their childhood in day-care settings, but few recall the outside environment as a special place of playful exploration. Some express a longing to leave our urban areas, to find those natural safe places that nurture us. Others plan to return to their families' native land, where they hope to provide experiences in the natural environment for their children, experiences they believe are now impossible to find in the urban areas of the United States.

Pathways   Youth are bounded by the dangers of urban traffic. Walks to and from school were once a time to explore water moving along a gutter, to take a shortcut past a favorite tree, or to discover a place to create a new secret hideaway. These routes are now determined by adults and confined by the necessary "escorts." Children are taken to school, soccer fields, parks, friend's homes; seldom are they empowered to journey on their own. According to research conducted by Hillman and associates (1990), in the 20 years between 1970 and 1990 the number of seven- and eight-year-olds permitted to go to school on their own dropped from 80 percent to 9 percent. This change represents a major impact on children's lifestyle; they are no longer experiencing the freedom to engage in a variety of activities or to pursue special interests in the out-of-doors (Titman 1994).

Urban Adventures   When the temperature drops and the wind's chill pierces layers of clothing, we go inside to find safe, warm places that we can predict and control with thermostats, log fires, more blankets, and hot tea. Weather today is beamed 24 hours a day on TV stations. We hear and see approaching hurricanes, tornadoes, ice storms, and heat waves. This increasing access to information about natural events can be contrasted with the growing unrest related to predicting human behavior, especially in our urban areas. Traffic impacts our cities, deadlocking streets and polluting our air. Poorly maintained streets and alleyways, where litter and graffiti dominate, are an indication of neglect that encourages dangerous activity. Street life is scary. Nine-, ten-, and eleven-year-olds' descriptions of urban Los Angeles, paint a picture of a place that is unsafe, unsightly, and unpredictable. "They [youth] say they are unable to freely occupy or explore their yards, their streets, their neighborhoods or communities" (Buss 1995, p. 350). At a time when these school-age children need to be out in the world with their peers, experiencing positive social and skill-building activities, they are instead experiencing a shrinking environment filled with serious and dangerous constraints.

Acts of violence underscore the realities of lack of control. We gather our children inside to find safe places we can count on. We create inside activities, using videos and television. Our youth are increasingly locked into controlled, limited, and scheduled indoor environments. Activities are usually passive and sight-dominated. When ways of learning about our world that involve smell, touch, and tase are confined and constrained, children miss the richness of direct, spontaneous, sensory feedback. A story is told (Zavitkovsky 1996) about children in a child care center who remained seated after a video had ended, staring intently at what seemed to be a blank screen. The teacher discovered, as she investigated, that everyone was absorbed in watching a small ant negotiating its way across the slippery glass of the screen. It was a slow journey for the tiny ant, and the children were relieved when it reached the other side. Although there is an important place for videos, computers, and television programs in educational environments, these must not overwhelm or replace our children's connections to living things. When connections with people, animals, or plants are made only by pushing buttons, learning by interacting with the real stuff of life—e.g., ants—is missing.

Connections

◆By design I mean conceiving and shaping complex systems. . . . Design in this sense requires reestablishing some connections that began coming loose in the Renaissance and were entirely severed by industrialization. The first connection to be reestablished is that between people and nature.

—Lyle 1994, p. ix

We are connected to people and places in a global environment through technology. An intimate view of life in remote, wild places permeates the television programming viewed in many homes. Children's T-shirts colorfully declare the importance of protecting rain forests and whales. Formal lessons learned in schools make up a familiar environmental vocabulary. Yet immediately outside the classroom—the inside space where concern for our ecosphere is being taught—is a wasteland of potentially rich soil covered with chemically produced asphalt. If children are learning about the connections between all living things, the interdependence of our ecosystem, the importance of caring for habitat, how is that concern reflected in their own outside habitat? If children are expected to learn about environmental issues, how can that happen in yards devoid of plant and animal life? Unfortunately, the connection a child might make is that adults teach one thing inside, but in the schoolyard, where he or she must spend part of their time every day, they do something else.

We see graffiti and are bothered by its presence. We pass a neglected park, littered pathways, chains dangling from structures that once were swings, broken drinking fountains, and assume that this physical environment indicates an ethos. We connect this evidence of lack of care for space as a symbol that the place and, perhaps, the people are not valued. Children too read school grounds, places they believe are essentially for them and their use. School grounds are physical symbols of the ways children's needs are understood and valued (Titman 1994).

> ✦To counter the historic trend toward the loss of wildness where children play, it is clear that we need to find ways to let children roam beyond the pavement, to gain access to vegetation and earth that allow them to tunnel, climb, or even fall. And because formal playgrounds are the only outdoors that many children experience anymore, shouldn't we be paying more attention to planting, and less to building on them?
> —G. Nabhan and S. Trimble 1994, p. 9

School grounds are the primary environments that provide children a chance to be connected to an outdoor environment on a regular basis. They are unlike any other outside public space, because the school environment is totally dedicated to children's use (Titman 1994). Going to school is an enforced experience. All children have access to school grounds regardless of the particular circumstances that may affect their lifestyle. In studies of fourth and fifth graders in urban Los Angeles, children describe the school as an oasis, a place where they still feel safe (Buss 1995). School grounds offer a special challenge to designers to get involved in the transformation of these outside spaces.

School Grounds as Outdoor Habitats

> ✦As the world becomes a more dangerous place and children's freedom to roam decreases, so the school grounds, as a safe open space, become ever more important—a special place for generations of special people.
> —Titman 1994, p. i

Recognizing that school grounds are probably the first public environment in which a child spends significant amounts of time, and that they are usually poorly designed expanses of hard surfaced material, Learning Through Landscapes (LTL) was formed in 1990 in United Kingdom. This unique organization deals with all aspects of school ground development, providing information, advice, research, training, and innovative projects. Its purpose is to "promote improvements to the environmental quality and educational use of school grounds by coordinating an imaginative program of activities designed to encourage sustainable developments" (*LTL Annual Report 1993–94*, p. 2). The organization began in the late 1980s with research projects that studied the design, use, and development of school grounds in the United Kingdom and other countries in Europe. One result of this study was the identification of the large educational estate in Britain encompassing more than 125,000 acres that schools own. Understanding the importance of this outdoor asset, a primary aim of the project was to assist schools in the transformation of their grounds for the benefit of children. The organization is guided by five principles, summarized as follows (Lucas 1995, p. 235):

1. *School grounds have a significant impact on children's development.*

2. *Any changes to school grounds, if they are to be successful, must involve the children.*

3. *Developing school grounds should be a "holistic" effort, meaning the widest possible involvement in the process and in the definition of the formal and informal and hidden curriculum that takes place there.*

4. *The development of a school ground is a multiprofessional activity (i.e., involving parents, children, teachers, administration, landscape architects, architects, artists, and ecologists).*

5. *School grounds should be developed in a sustainable way.*

A part of the Learning Through Landscapes project is a special program, the Urban Challenge, focused on complex environmental problems that impact the inner-city schools. Creating an oasis in the urban environment is encouraged by financial awards. In order to receive these award funds, schools submit applications of projects that demonstrate specific solutions to each school's particular needs. A staff at a Liverpool school describes the program and its award incentive as, "seeing things growing in places where you just didn't think they could grow" (Learning Through Landscapes 1995, p. 13). The award criteria for a school's project include commitment of the whole school and its community to the project, active pupil involvement, evidence of a long-term management plan, incorporation of the project into the school development plan, and commitment to document the project for the benefit of others (Learning Through Landscapes 1995, p. 12). The program also provides financial awards to help schools get their projects started. As one of LTL's many projects, Urban Challenge recognizes the importance of supporting positive change in inner-city school grounds where the impact of social problems is often most intense.

The following case studies describe the transformation of four outside school grounds. An elementary school in Cambridgshire, United Kingdom, is an illustration of redesigning a school's outside property using Learning Through Landscape's five basic principles. The second study tells the story of teenagers, administration, faculty, and graduate design students working together to redesign their high school's central courtyard. The process was guided by student and faculty concern that this outside social gathering area should better support the students' social needs and, at the same time, consider the student body's concern for environmental issues and sustainability. This is a story of empowering teenagers through a participatory design process. The third case study describes how children and families were involved in designing and transforming their physical environment, a participatory activity based on the school's history and the valuing of community building. In this prekindergarten/elementary school, even the youngest participated in planning their playground transformation from what was known as a "dog run" to a special place. The final study describes a vacant lot at a public elementary school in a highly transient area of a southern California city. Envisioning a project that might turn a vacant lot into a garden for children and the surrounding neighborhood, the principal worked with the manager of a local horticulture therapy and adult training program. The adults in training, adjacent neighbors, and elementary school children and staff are all working together to create a "magical garden" that is a source of pride to the neighborhood and a model for other residents in the city.

CASE STUDY
Coton Community Primary School
Coton, Cambridgeshire, United Kingdom

A visitor to Coton Community Primary School, who has taught for many years in the United States, introduces the first study. Mary shares her initial reaction as she relates the visual impact of the school grounds on her thinking. Her remarks are followed by the case study written by head teacher Ruth Poulton, who describes the design and development of the school grounds using the support and guidelines of the Learning Through Landscapes project.

Mary:
I've seen it! Coton Community Primary School is the most inspiring example of outdoor environmental design taken to heart. Being told that the school was just across the road from the church, which dates back to 1377,

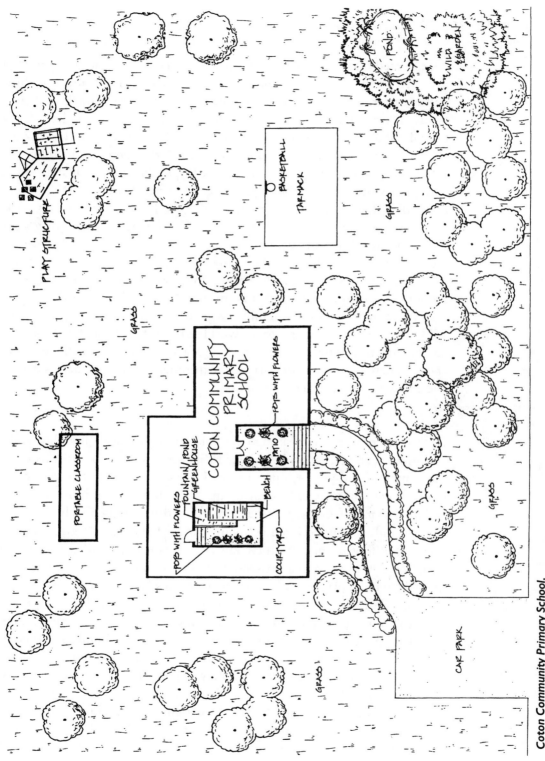

Coton Community Primary School.

School grounds showing wild lands, enclosed weather patio, and location of children's play structure.

I anticipated that history would also be embodied in the school building—I assumed a very old, unique, and interesting structure. I imagined the difficulties that must have been encountered in creating a modern school. Much to my surprise, that is just what Coton school building is—modern. It is a typical compact single story, flat-topped brick structure, graced with very large windows encircling the entire building. In the center of the school, is a courtyard. My first impression of another typical institution-like structure was quickly displaced by the impact of all the trees sheltering the grounds. More than 25 trees grow out front, creating the feel of a favorite city park. Some are delicate saplings, others majestic in their size. A swath of grasses begins at High Street and winds back into an open space as far as the eye can see. The walk up to the school's main entrance took me past a garden that was tidy, but not groomed. The shrubs and flowers grew freely, preparing me for the sense of freedom that permeates the school and wooden flower boxes lent their welcome. A child-designed wind vane and sun dial and a wild garden led me further into the world of Learning Through Landscapes, convincing me that the building structure of a school is only half of the school at best. There is a treasure of learning environments waiting to be discovered and created outside the classroom door.

Ruth:

I began my headship 11 years ago in a small rural primary school one and a half miles west of Cambridge, United Kingdom. The school is situated in the center of the village, opposite St. Peter's Church, and has an open interface with the village. A public footpath ran along the western boundary, and the grounds were used by the community during out- of-school hours. The grounds comprised a gently sloping playing field behind the school, the only uphill football pitch in the county, a netball court/hard surfaced play area, flower borders, and a grassed area to the front of the school. Between the field and the playground there was a glorious bank of trees, providing a rich variety of texture and color, in addition to welcome shade from the sun during summer playtimes. Although this was a pleasant environment, there wasn't anything to stimulate curiosity or to challenge the pupils. I wanted to change the grounds into a place to foster play, to develop pupils' spirit of adventure, to encourage informal learning, and to act as a resource for formal learning.

At this time there was no National Curriculum in the United Kingdom and teachers were free to plan their own programs. I decided on a project based on the theme "adventure." We studied adventurers in history and considered the question, "What is the 'spirit of adventure'?" The children decided that it meant meeting a challenge, and so we looked at the challenges that face pupils in their lives.

> *I think it is dangerous, full of excitement, discovery, and courage. It is exploring, meeting challenges, and alertness. There is always something new, something with great awe and wonder and power, but a slight bit apprehensive.*
>
> —John James, age 10

> *Adventure is to experience a very exciting way to view, not only the world, but to test and challenge yourself to a limit.*
>
> —Anna Mason, age 10

In science we studied structures and strong shapes. We considered physical challenge, and each pupil designed an adventure structure that could be built outside to provide that challenge. I made two specifications. The first was that the structure had to be unique. I explained that this must not be like any structure they had seen before. The second consideration was that the structure should enclose a central creative play space where children could use their imagination to create anything they might want the structure to represent—a boat, a fort, a hideout, etc. Each student drew designs of his or her own ideas. From these ideas the pupils made models of structures, and we presented these to the parent-teacher association in the hope that the

A play area based on the theme of "Adventure" developed with children at the Coton School.
(Photo by Ruth Poulton.)

parents might raise the funds to build some of the pupils' own designs. We spent two terms fundraising, during which time we were very fortunate to meet a sculptor, Christine Fox, who took the children's models to her art class students. She showed them to six young adults who created a working plan for the structure by incorporating the children's design ideas. The overall design was like a maze. By this time we had raised sufficient money to build half the design. Problems are simplified if they are broken down into manageable parts, and so we prepared to build stage one.

A date was set for a working weekend, and I asked the parents to decide which tools they would be willing to bring along. We needed to hire a post hole auger and a concrete mixer. In the meantime, the six art students were working on some of the upright posts and carving their tops with creatures, for example, an owl, a monkey, an octopus, etc. During the week before, the 10- and 11-year-old pupils set out the form of the maze using pegs and string. They also marked the ground where all the upright supports would be fixed.

There was great excitement on the Saturday work commenced. A good diverse labor force turned up, composed of parents, teachers, pupils, Christine, and her six students. Each parent was assigned two Coton children to work with, and we set about digging holes, stripping bark, and treating the wood with preservatives. Unfortunately, we didn't know about tanalysing wood (non toxic treatment) then. I cooked a barbecue lunch for everyone, and we completed this first stage and arranged a grand opening. The children had a new outside resource, one they had been involved with from the beginning brainstorming stages to the final building. Because of their involvement they had a strong sense of ownership.

The following year we repeated the process. The theme this time was "movement." We studied people who moved around, such as the nomads, or the scientific movement of the body as a physical organism. We decided that we wanted to be able to balance, swing, climb, slide, jump, and run. The children continued to create design ideas, and we worked again with adult art students and parents. Together we built stage two. As a community of many ages and talents, we realized on completion that together we had created an aesthetically pleasing design and added to the resources available outside on the school grounds.

I felt that the Coton staff was working in isolation until I met Eileen Adams, who was studying the design, use, and management of the land surrounding school buildings in England and Wales. Her work was a part of the newly developing Learning Through Landscapes project. Following Adams's final report in 1990, the Learning Through Landscapes Trust was established to implement its recommendations. The Trust brought together teachers who independently had been developing their own school grounds. Now they began to share experiences, expertise, and research. We all believed that the quality of the outside school environment and the quality of learning and social activity that take place in it constitute a key relationship.

Meanwhile, back at Coton we had embarked on a planting plan to enrich the soft landscape. Using various professionals in the field, along with the children's ideas, a variety of plant materials were chosen. With the children we set a beech hedge to the west, in anticipation of those glorious colors, a buddleia hedge to attract butterflies, and a hedge of "Old English" plants endemic to Cambridgeshire. Several trees were also added to the school's boundaries.

We have learned much since those early days. Our current goal is to complete an audit of the school grounds and to formulate a long term development plan with input from many sectors, rather like a wish list. We want to avoid future development problems by being sensitive to a process of change and considering the whole over time, rather than pieces in our immediate future.

We began the audit of our school grounds with a mathematics activity whereby groups of pupils measured the site and produced a scale plan of the school building and its outside space. We studied the hedgerows and identified all the plants in those hedges. We identified the trees and marked them on the scale plan. Eventually, we gathered all the relevant information about position, surrounding land and its use, wildlife sharing our grounds, and our adjacent community. With this information we were able to begin long term planning. We chose a simple beginning to introduce two new varieties of tree per year, thus ensuring involvement of successive classes. To initiate an awareness of the grounds from the beginning, the youngest (reception or kindergarten) pupils planted bulbs. Simple tasks engaged everyone in environmental awareness.

The next project we embarked on was to create a wild garden. As a staff, we brainstormed the possibilities and set down our aims for this project. We had learned from our previous experiences that problems are most easily solved if broken down into achievable tasks. For this project, each class developed a different aspect of the garden: a pond, some nesting boxes, a bird hide, wildflowers, places for hedgehogs or mini-beasts. The tasks associated with creating a pond involved a variety of mathematics activities. One class investigated the problems of measuring the distance from the nearest water source to the pond and purchased the required hose pipe.

A wild garden with a small pond attracts a variety of wildlife on the Coton school grounds.
(Photo by Ruth Poulton.)

Places for adults to sit outside always seem to be in short supply in schools, and special spaces on school grounds that encourage children to sit and share secrets are usually missing. We set about building seating. This project was a part of a broader study involving trees, wood, paper, and printing. Toward the end of the project, I brought a range of materials into the classroom, together with a builder's catalog. The children made models of their ideas. I invited a man from the builder's merchants to come and help the children cost their plans.

The next stage was to evaluate the childrens' designs. We discussed the criteria for evaluation, and the children offered the following suggestions: (1) function—does it do the job? (2) form—shape, design, originality aesthetics (3) ease of construction—can we build it? and (4) cost—can we afford it? The pupils displayed their models and plans. Each numbered design was evaluated by the students and teachers, who scored zero to five against the four criteria. We selected two designs to build.

The most recent project is the development of the school's courtyard. The nine- to eleven-year-olds sat in the space and brainstormed ideas to make this area more interesting. We transformed a bleak inner courtyard into a special place by making a solar powered fountain and a sun dial and adding a wind vane, plants, and sculptures.

Pupils used the theme of "gods and goddesses" as inspiration for the artifacts in the weather garden. We studied the phases of the moon. From the pupil's drawings, nine moons were chosen to use for sculpture patterns. Christine Fox cut these out of aluminum, and the children beat their patterns into them using a sand tray. The forms were completed by painting them with translucent blue ink.

Phases of the moon enhance the facade of the school building in this courtyard.
(Photo by Ruth Poulton.)

A greenhouse with a solar panel used to power a small adjacent fountain.
(Photo by Ruth Poulton.)

An old greenhouse was moved into the courtyard. A grapevine was planted, and pots made by the children were placed around the pond. Before we could design the fountain, we located a small solar panel, which we taped onto the south-facing side of the greenhouse roof. The sound of running water helps to make the courtyard a special place. We started to collect edible and medicinal plants to grow in the flower beds or in the greenhouse and tree nursery.

Pupils, parents, teachers, and members of Coton community all worked together to create this weather garden that fills the interior of our school with soft plants, soothing sounds, art, and nature and is a place for continuing creative educational activities. Our future plans include creating a geological rock garden, building an outdoor stage, making a storyteller's chair, revamping the wild garden, and building an adventure trail around the entire perimeter of the school grounds.

For the past five years I have been running a county network to promote and support landscape development on school grounds in Cambridgeshire. We meet together to share ideas and good practice, sometimes learning from each other's mistakes. The pond we built in our wild garden taught us about many problems that others have since avoided! Conferences are arranged to bring expertise to our members from the National Learning through Land-

A snake sculpture fountain and pond create a soothing space in a formerly empty, hard school courtyard.
(Photo by Ruth Poulton.)

A sundial based on the Coton School children's study of solar time.
(Photo by Ruth Poulton.)

scape Trust. We have a directory of local experts who will give their time freely to support schools.

The school grounds are often the first place that pupils, parents, and visitors see, and impressions about a school may be formed even before entering the building. The grounds communicate messages in a unique way and their contribution to the atmosphere of the school is significant, as this

Children pot various plants to eventually enrich the natural feeling of their school courtyard.
(Photo by Ruth Poulton.)

A child-designed weather
vane for Coton Community
School.

(Photo by Ruth Poulton.)

environment reflects the values and attitudes of the people who work there. School grounds are among the few areas in which schools are free to develop their individuality.

Participation

◆You don't give up your role as a designer. That's an erroneous thought about participatory design from the '60s. It's our responsibility to take these [children's] ideas and turn them into options.

—Goltsman, in Leccesse 1995, p. 73

Empowering Youth Children may do all the running or collecting or selling to raise money for a school event, but often have little or no say in the way a project is chosen or the way funds are spent. Children may be consulted or have voting power, but too often their creative ideas, dreams, and concerns never deepen the adults' view of a project. Feedback about how an environment actually works for children is seldom solicited (Baldassari, Lehman, and Wolfe, 1987). Young people need to develop their abilities to investigate ideas and brainstorm solutions as part of growing up in a world where our planet's environmental dilemmas will demand complex problem-solving processes and collective decision making (Moore 1990).

Adults' understanding of outside school areas can be enriched by seriously involving children in assessment, planning, and design so that their input helps guide physical change. This participation reaps benefits beyond the value of developing a more appropriate design for the user (Hart 1992). When children and youth are provided with opportunities to be active participants in a design process, where they share ideas and decisions with the adults who have power, it is evidence that the school trusts and values them (Titman 1994). Working together to redesign the courtyard at Rosemead High School, teenagers, staff, administration, and graduate design students experienced the creativity, fun, and pride of a shared participatory design process. The case study that follows tells their story.

CASE STUDY
Rosemead High School, Rosemead, California

Thirty miles directly east of the urban core of Los Angeles, next to the Interstate 10 freeway is Rosemead High School. Built in 1949 during the post-World War II housing boom, it originally served a growing suburban population in adjacent neighborhoods of small-single family, middle-class homes and apartment complexes. During its 50 years, the high school has experienced the same changing trends evident in the greater Los Angeles area school system. A large influx of Pacific Rim families, immigrants from many Southeast Asian lands, and families fleeing political or economic crisis in countries south of our border account for a growing population of Asian and Hispanic students.

Although there have been dramatic changes in the cultural and ethnic backgrounds of RHS students, over the past 40 years the physical environment has changed very little. Lockers still line the long hallways and slam with the same echoing sound as students rush to class. The Senior Patio is still a highly symbolic area for those who will be graduating within the year. Panther Square is still the primary place students congregate. Pep rallies, drill team practice, hanging out with friends, gathering over a quick lunch, and watching others to learn more about yourself still happen in outside social gathering areas on this campus.

Rosemead High was originally built as a showpiece in the Los Angeles area with strict adherence to Streamline Modern Style. Although the overall design of the campus has changed very little over the years, the school's

The drill team practices in Panther Square at Rosemead High School.

physical environment, both buildings and grounds, deteriorated in the 1970s because of diminishing funds available from traditional sources. Drainage, storage, poor lighting, faded paint, seriously eroded plant material, and heating and cooling problems were a few of the issues needing attention.

In the early 1980s there began a concerted effort to restore the school's image (Anthony 1987). Air conditioning, painting, repairs, new furnishings, and better lighting have all added to an increased sense of pride in the school buildings. However, the outside area, in particular the central courtyard known as Panther Square, has experienced a loss of trees and an increase in the overall amount of asphalt. Former planted areas were paved over to save maintenance and repair costs. Realizing that attention needed to be directed

Few natural spots remain in the high school gathering area, except for space adjacent to the "senior wall."

to refurbishing the outside area of the high school, RHS administration contacted the Landscape Architecture program at California State Polytechnic University, Pomona. Graduate students in both architecture and landscape architecture, along with their faculty, spent two quarters working with RHS students, faculty, and staff. They sought a better understanding of the problems and possibilities in the use of the school's outside space, primarily Panther Square. Together they generated plans and ideas for future changes.

Forty high school students elected by their classmates, representing all four years, met with eight graduate landscape architecture and architecture students enrolled in a Human Factors and Design class. Gathered together in a small room filled with large cafeteria-style tables, they began "breaking the ice," by making playful name tags for each other, discovering favorite things to do, see, and eat, describing favorite places to be. These graduate students, not much older then the teenagers themselves, represented a similar make-up of Asian/Pacific and Mexican family heritage. They had much in common, including a taste for take-out pizza, generously provided by the school's vice principal, which they shared at the conclusion of the workshops. They discovered that they also shared a concern about ecological issues, and everyone agreed that any changes to Panther Square should consider sustainability as a guide.

High school students begin to inventory their site, taking awareness walks as a first step in the redesign process for Panther Square.

Working in teams, high school students begin to express their ideas about their outside gathering area.

Using the "Take Part" process developed by Jim Burns (1979) as a model, small groups explored the existing outside space through a series of "awareness walks" (Burns and Halprin 1974). Cognitive maps became colorful red (dislike) and green (like) sticker collections of descriptive information about Panther Square from the teens' point of view. The large tables were covered with yards of butcher paper filled with RHS students' ideas of ways to transform the outside core of their high school. Each small group, in turn, presented these ideas to the larger group. The graduate students were amazed at the sustained level of interest, complexity of problem solving skills, analytical thinking, and fun that everyone shared.

To reach a wider range of student input, the graduate students put together and circulated a survey among the student body. RHS students were asked to describe how they currently used the outside space, to rate various existing elements in Panther Square, and to make prioritized suggestions for change. Faculty were also surveyed at this time. As a final information-gath-

Groups brainstorm what they need in Panther Square.

ering tool, focused interviews were completed with administration and maintenance staff. Throughout the study, the graduate students continued to observe and record the ways the teenagers used Panther Square.

Sharing another noontime take-out pizza, the graduate students met with the 40 student representatives, school administrators, and some faculty and staff members. They summarized the many things they had learned from the RHS students. The results of their work were presented and then tabulated, described, and printed in a booklet for the students and staff at the high school. They described concept plans and suggested a design to change Panther Square. The teens saw their ideas take form. Comfort, maintenance, and aesthetics, three elements the teenagers described as major issues, were used as guiding concepts in the design process. Seating, shade, site furnishings, improved surfaces, painting, signage, drainage, vegetation, grass, color, and trash were elements that all agreed must be addressed.

Because the high school students expressed concerned about environmental issues, sustainability guided the graduate students' thinking and final conceptual design (Lyle 1994). Catchment of rainwater on site during the often heavy winter storms influenced the design of the more intimate seating areas. Plant selection was based on the possible ecological role of vegetation, such as filtering the air in this heavily polluted part of California.

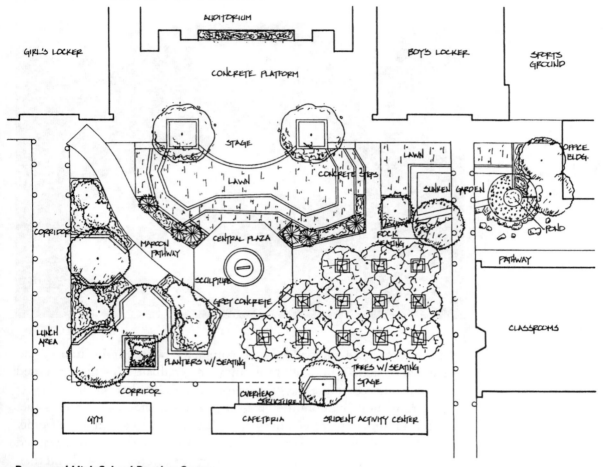

Rosemead High School Panther Square.
Proposed design completed with teenagers and graduate students enrolled in Landscape Architecture at California State Polytechnic University in Pomona.

Students also expressed the importance of symbols that make their high school unique and special. The senior class mural, which is repainted each June by the graduating class, and the lone pine tree were recognized as landmarks and incorporated and enhanced in the suggested changes to the square. The graduate students created new design elements, based on the teenagers' desire to use the school colors and mascot, to create an outdoor setting with meaning for this particular high school.

Using these drawings, the administration took the opportunity to begin fundraising to make outside space changes a reality. Initial support began when an RHS alumnus in the nursery business volunteered to donate plants, and another alumnus in construction work offered his services. The RHS

RHS shop teacher led his class in the building of a model based on the plan view design completed by the Cal Poly students. The local newspaper wrote a story about the school's efforts, and donations continued to flow from the local community and alumni. The school community is working to turn the ideas of their youth into options that will transform the heart of their school, Panther Square, into a gathering place where teens have a sense of ownership and pride.

> ✦*Research conducted throughout the world consistently finds that the involvement of children and young people in projects leads to a sense of responsibility for the maintenance, care and protection of that which has been created.*
>
> —Titman 1994, p. 88

Building Community The following case study describes a community of families who were faced with relocating their school after being housed in a church basement for 18 years. In 1990 the school was given three months to box up everything and move to another site. During the following transitional year and a half, the parents and staff moved their school three times. Finally locating a potential site, the community worked together to purchase the property and then recycle what had been a china factory into a new setting to house Walden School. Carol Per Lee, who directs the school, tells the story. It begins with parents, staff, and children planning, designing, and actually doing some of the remodeling work to transform the china factory into a school. The story continues with a description of the process of changing the adjacent outside spaces into places to play. Community building through participation of even the youngest three-year-olds is a continuing theme and focus of this story.

CASE STUDY
Walden School, Pasadena, California

Carol:

Our quest began in 1970 with two parents who wanted a different learning environment for their children. The school they formed quickly outgrew the home where it was originally located and moved into a rented lower level of a nearby church. This particular church site was chosen because a large city park lay directly across the street, providing an inviting play area for the children's space-bound exuberance contained by the building. Over the years the seventy children and eight staff members became used to the lack of light and small spaces as they creatively improvised, using every available nook and cranny to create a setting for learning.

After 18 years our school was notified in September that the church was no longer interested in leasing its space and we were asked, "Oh, by the way, could you be out in December?" We were faced with closure! We had never conducted a feasibility study or a capital campaign, nor were there rental spaces nearby to permit current families to continue attending. A parent meeting was held and we considered our options: close the school; locate another rental space somewhere; figure out a way to buy a site. Families' commitment to the school and its philosophy to nurture a child's natural wonder and personal dignity was the most important factor. They pooled their collective resources and brainstormed their contacts. Within three months they accomplished what many would consider impossible.

In order to complete the school year, an abandoned school site 10 miles away was rented. Despite the dilapidated condition of the buildings, the grounds were incredibly spacious, providing trees to climb safely and open spaces in which to play. We all managed the extra commute and the leaky roofs with cascading water just outside my door.

Only two miles from our original church location was a ceramics plant/art studio housed in an industrial concrete block structure. The brothers who owned the building were retiring and wanted to sell. Touched by the school's predicament, and the determination of the parents, the owners were willing to work with creative financing for purchase. Walden is fortunate to have an architect, an owner of a construction company, and two lawyers among its community of families. The parents, none of whom were particularly wealthy, worked to raise the $250,000 down payment, to redesign and rebuild the factory with no budget reserves, and to double the school enrollment for a site "unseen" by prospective families. Three months later they had managed to collect the down payment loans (none greater than $10,000) and had a first draft of the building plan with construction tasks outlined. Everyone got involved. Pregnant moms, dads who had never knocked down walls before, grandparents and friends all pitched in to build their school. Fifteen months after the church originally asked us to vacate, we opened at our own site.

During the next six years we worked to pay back all of our loans and to complete the final phases of the original remodeling plan. The outside play yards remained the major areas that needed transformation. Known as North and South Yards, these long rectilinear concrete areas were filled with

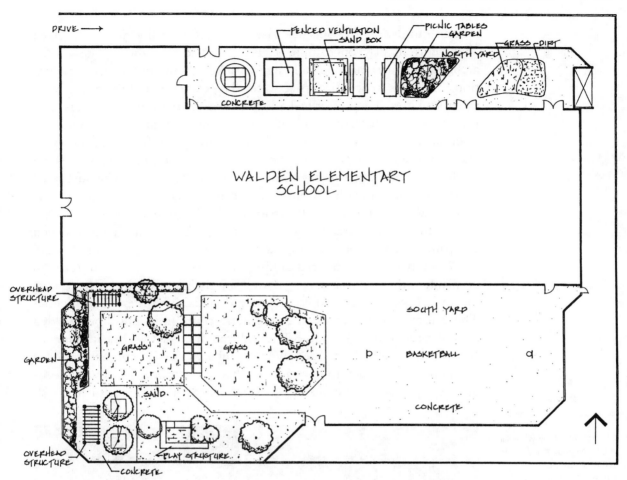

Walden School North and South Yards.
North Yard, current site where evaluation and planning is taking place with school community.

problems: too hot in the sunny months, too cold in wet weather, hard surfaces edged by the concrete block building and school fencing, no natural elements, few possibilities for play except ball games. The outdoors offered our children sameness and certainly did not meet one of the school goals as expressed in our Mission Statement, "To teach that we all have stewardship for the world in which we live."

We began to work on ideas for South Yard. Each of the eight classes selected two of their members to be on a planning team to discuss the yards. The children were chosen for their "fair-mindedness as well as their ability to help solve problems." Sixteen children, ages five to twelve, met four times a month to discuss the outside space problems as well as what they liked about current play opportunities. They studied the initial plans of the architect who designed the building. We talked about the childrens' frustrations, the ways to organize space so that ball games wouldn't conflict with other activities. They described a longing for natural things, the grass and trees they love. I took the children's suggestions to the architect and held an assembly to report our work to the whole school. Children had nacho sale, and staff sought foundation support. At the school's annual auction we held a "Grass Roots" campaign in which a square yard of sod could be purchased for the school yard with a twenty-five dollar donation. With some funding in place, we began phase one. Two parents, a landscape architect, and a curator at the Huntington Garden Desert Collection, joined with the construction company owner to help us complete the transformation of our South Yard.

When two specimen-sized camphor trees were trucked in and ready to be planted, the children prepared well for their successful growth. That morning I went around to each class and talked with the children about Thoreau and his thoughts on ecology and community and how Walden School came to have its name. The children discussed wishes and dreams and how they could be realized. We remembered how parents and children had hoped for Walden to have a new school site and the work we accomplished together. Each child and staff member then wrote his or her wish

Children toss their wishes into the hole excavated for the school's new tree.
(Photo by Carol Per Lee.)

The long rectilinear shape and hard surfaces provide challenges in the redesign of Walden School's North Yard.

Children describe their favorite play spaces to university design students.

for the new yard, and for the school as a community. We placed our wishes at the bottom of the holes just before the two new trees were planted. Walden now has two Wishing Trees to remind us of how wishes come to be. One child in the second-third grade class exclaimed, "Wouldn't it be neat if when the leaves fall, we could hear the whispers of the wishes underneath?"

We still faced a major challenge—to redesign our North Yard. This small space used by the youngest children, three to five years old, was characterized by a prospective parent as a "glorified dog run." Most of us agreed, but constrained by traffic needs to the north and a four- by eight-foot fenced ventilation system near the center of this fully cemented space, constructive solutions for providing an inviting play area eluded us.

Graduate design student listens to child's play activity ideas.

Children gather at an outside table to make drawings expressing their thoughts and feelings about play.

A landscape architect, a member of Walden School's Advisory Board, suggested involving her college students currently studying community design issues. Ten students began working at Walden School to fulfill their current class project requirement. In order to be sensitive to the developmental needs of the youngest children, the college students divided themselves into three small teams. Each team "adopted" two classes and although they approached their groups of children somewhat differently, everyone began by observing and followed with getting- acquainted games with the children. The college students planned a variety of activities to encourage the children's expression, both verbally and in art form. A visualization exercise, going outside to find disliked areas or objects, drawing favorite play activities, and hunting for things they never noticed before were among

Making a large mural, children are involved drawing things they like and dislike outside.

the activities that engaged the children. Murals, discussions, group sharing, and one-on-one interviews were all a part of the process.

The children described a general range of "liked" activities, from computer games to sitting in quiet shady places, from hiding in the bushes along the side of my house to going to the Disneyland castle. All of these children described the same problems in their yard and related similar wishes for their play area. They wanted more interesting options for physical activities, imaginatively drawing things like a "tricycle slide." Every group of children mentioned natural elements such as trees and flowers, with bugs, slugs, worms, ladybugs and spiders in the mud and under rocks. They complained about physical discomfort: It's too hot when its sunny, too cold in the winter, too wet if it rains; the sand hurts when it gets on the concrete and makes you fall. The five- and six-year-olds clearly described problems of scale: Every-

Apple trees, a book, and a little seat represent a child's dream for a school yard.

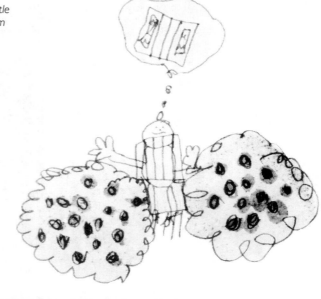

Bugs, worms, and other critters are a child's favorite things outside.

thing was too small—the trike path, the playhouse, the plastic climbing structure. The children's feelings, descriptions, and evaluations became the treasures the community began to mine. The college students learned about the importance of involving even the very young as valued and contributing members of a school's community.

◆*The garden has become an instrument of power that enables them to make the neighborhood safer and more beautiful. The garden also holds the power to restore their faith in themselves and in nature.*
—Severson 1993, p. 80

Involving Neighborhoods Just as a living plant sends our roots and branches as it grows, so the transformation of school outdoor spaces is a process that can reach out into the adjacent neighborhood. The case study that follows describes such reaching out. Seeing an opportunity to involve neighbors with their local school, an elementary school principal envisioned a garden on the school's property— originally a weed filled lot, a place where people discarded not

Even the young three-year-olds are involved in the design of their outside yard.

only objects but their pride. The project branched beyond the immediate families to include a local horticulture therapy program involved in providing training for people with disabilities. They are now working together—the neighbors, the school children, and staff, and the adults in training—to transform an outside space at a public elementary school into an "instrument of power."

CASE STUDY
Lincoln Elementary School, Pomona, California

The vacant lot between the school building and the parking area was an eyesore—an weed-filled, rocky, and sometimes litter-strewn area. The school principal, Amaury Rodriguez, decided that turning this area into a garden could become a symbol to the residents of Gordon Street . He believed that such a project would build community in this very transient area. The children who attend Lincoln Elementary School come from the neighborhood; however, there is a 50 percent turnover every year. The principal knew that the residents of the nearby apartment houses had no access to land or to growing plants. However, he believed that children

Lincoln School's vacant property is being developed by the community as a garden. The Living Teepee structure is just beginning to grow.

should understand ecology and learn to care for nature, not just from books in classrooms, but outside with real plants.

Through a grant from the California Community Foundation to the Pomona Council of Churches to fund community empowerment projects, Lincoln School as part of the Gordon Street Coalition received financial resources to begin its garden project. At the same time, Paul Alderson, the division manager of a horticulture therapy and training program for adults with disabilities, contacted the Council of Churches seeking ways to broaden the range of community work sites for his clients. He had been running this program at the University Ornamental Horticulture Unit for the past five years. Recently his staff had been broadening the range of places where their clients are based. This project seemed like a perfect match. The adults with disabilities could work with the school and neighborhood to create gardens. The local newspaper reported the beginnings of this project.

> The signs of a fragmented community show up in many places in Pomona, from vandal-stricken neighborhoods to the city's homicide rate, which now sits at 10 people dead in just the first two months of the year. But last weekend, more than fifty people from one Pomona neighborhood gathered together in an effort to strengthen the ties that bind the community together. They didn't picket or protest the recent spate of violence, they simply planted in peace.
>
> Neighborhood residents and city officials joined students at Lincoln Elementary School on Saturday, despite the wet weather, to break ground on a community garden that will serve as a creative focal point for the Gordon Street neighborhood. Paul Alderson, the division manager of Casa Colina's Horticulture Training program is coordinating the project. He described work crews descending on an undeveloped lot adjoining the school to dig up weeds, clear rocks, and prep the raw earth for phased planting. Over time he said the garden will evolve and be transformed by the imaginations of the children at the school. "As they grow and change, so will the garden," said Alderson.
>
> —Pomona Valley News, 9 March 1995

Principles and practices agreed upon by the Gordon Street Coalition and Lincoln Elementary School guide the design and development of the garden. One of these is to model interdependence with "no borders, fences or squares, . . . cycles and circles of interdependence and creative relationships will unify and identify with the garden structure" (Principles and Practices of the Gordon Street Coalition, 1996). Even though a person can cultivate his or her own small piece of land for 12 dollars a year, edges are difficult to

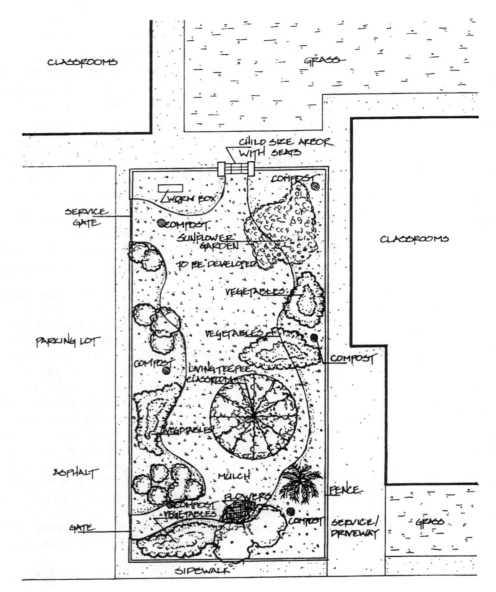

CLASSROOMS

GRASS

CHILD SIZE ARBOR WITH SEATS

COMPOST

WORM BOX

SERVICE GATE

COMPOST

SUNFLOWER GARDEN

TO BE DEVELOPED

CLASSROOMS

VEGETABLES

VEGETABLES

PARKING LOT

COMPOST

LIVING TEEPEE CLASSROOM

COMPOST

VEGETABLES

ASPHALT

MULCH

FLOWERS

FENCE

COMPOST VEGETABLES

COMPOST

SERVICE/ DRIVEWAY

GRASS

GATE

SIDEWALK

GORDON STREET

Lincoln Elementary School Magical Garden.
Vacant lot that children, teachers, and adjacent neighbors are transforming into their community garden.

Community members create
their own special signs for their
garden .

determine; the pathways curve, and unique hand-crafted signs mark a person's belief more than claim a specific garden plot.

The garden is growing an outdoor classroom based on the beanpole teepee ideas of Sharon Lovejoy (1991). It is a landmark not only for the school but for the neighborhood. Paul, who is also an artist, enjoys stimulating a garden design process by asking the question, "What if there were no limits?" The 30-foot-high beanpole teepee is one result of this kind of community brainstorming.

An entrance on the eastern edge of the garden, located adjacent to the classrooms, is built at child scale. This arbor with smaller benches welcomes children to their special garden. Compost bins, native plants, a sunflower habitat, the brilliant red of swiss chard and the yellow of squash visually

A child scale entrance leads from classrooms into the garden area.

Classroom buildings are adjacent to the garden.

A sunflower habitat is a tangible symbol of a community working together to transform Lincoln School's outside space.

demonstrate the rich variey of nature's process and are an example of ways we nurture living things. The garden, as part of the school grounds, can be read by the children and the neighborhood as a tangible symbol of the ways people care.

The school's principal continues to cultivate garden involvement with teachers and their students. Every Friday morning during the year, children can experience the garden as a doing/learning place. The students are joined by adults, who may also enroll in the classes. It is expected that the Friday class will attract older retired members of the neighborhood. The horticulture therapy program adults also attend the Friday classes, working side by side in the garden with the elementary school children and the neighbors. A class has been organized for one Saturday each month, open to everyone in the community. Court-refered youth work in the garden during these Saturday classes. As they continue to create their outside space, the children, youth, and adults are trying to understand how they can "empower human relationships . . . to provide a place of community and collaboration, and . . . encourage 'home grown' culture between people as well as plants in their garden" (Principles and Practices of the Gordon Street Coalition, 1996).

Design Over Time

✦*To make a meaningful place requires a shared understanding among designers, managers, and users. The structure of such a place will be given by the human purposes it serves, but its meaning will derive from the subtle poetics of time and place.*

—Carr et al. 1992

This book is an invitation to reenter those educational environments where children and youth are spending their lives. Standing in hard, boring, uninspired places, it is easy to imagine human sensitivities growing dull with the gray sameness of it all. Such stereotypical school grounds are a wasted resource. Here lies the challenge to change these places with an enhanced vision of what outside environments can become.

As this twentieth century spins into its last few days, we are bombarded by problems, by pressures to produce, by demands to hurry, to jam too much into tight-fitting daily routines that are the familiar clothing of this era. It is difficult to see things happening over time. We have become product oriented, completion bound, solution driven, rather than process involved.

To discover where to go in the approaching twenty-first century, we can begin by shedding the tight, familiar preconceptions that constrict our thinking. We can rethink the products of our routines and envision the playful exploration that could be possible outside the classroom door for our children who will live in the next millennium. We can discover ways to change school grounds so that our young people can daily connect to their earth. We can anticipate a future where the messages and meanings children gain from the design of their outside places inform them that we understand and support who they are and the many ways they learn . Encouraging experimentation, focusing on process, involving our younger people as equal partners in making changes and creating possibilities can move us toward a future where our educational institutions become meaningful particular places that grow over time through the creative interaction between children, educators, and designers.

References

Adams, Eileen. 1991. "Back to basics: Aesthetic experience." *Children's Environments Quarterly* 8(2): 19–29.

Anthony, Kathryn H. 1987. "Environment-behavior research applied to design: the case of Rosemead High School." *The Journal of Architectural and Planning Research* 4(2): 91–107.

Baldassari, Carol, Sheila Lehman, and Maxine Wolfe. 1987. "Imaging and creating alternative environments with children." In *Spaces for Children: The Built Environment and Child Development*, edited by C. Weinstein and T. David. New York: Plenum Press.

Bartlett, Sheridan. 1991. "Kids aren't like they used to be: Nostalgia and reality in neighborhood life." *Children's Environments Quarterly* 8(1): 49–58.

Burns, Jim and Lawrence Halprin. 1974. *Taking Part: A Workshop Approach to Collective Creativity*. Cambridge, MA: MIT Press.

Burns, Jim. 1979. *Connections: Ways to Discover and Realize Community Potential*. San Francisco, CA: McGraw-Hill.

Buss, Shirl. 1995. "Urban Los Angeles from young people's angle of vision." *Children's Environments* 12(3): 340–351.

Carr, Stephen, Mark Francis, Leanne Rivlin, and Andrew Stone. 1992. *Public Space*. New York: Cambridge University Press.

Christoffel, Katherine K. 1995. "Handguns and the environments of children." *Children's Environments* 12(1): 39–48.

Francis, Mark. 1995. "Childhood's garden: Memory and meaning of gardens." *Children's Environments* 12(2): 183–191.

Hart, Roger. 1992. *Children's Participation: From Tokenism to Citizenship—Innocenti Essays*. No. 4. New York: UNICEF.

Hillman, M., J. Adams, and J. Witlegg. 1990. *One False Move . . . A Study of Children's Independent Mobility*. London: The Policy Studies Institute.

Huttenmoser, Marco. 1995. "Children and their living surrounds: Empirical investigations into the significance of living surroundings for the everyday life and development of children." *Children's Environments* 12(4): 403–413.

Learning Through Landscapes. 1995. "E-scape." *Learning Through Landscapes Newsletter* 8 (June).

Leccese, Michael. 1995. "Redefining the idea of play." *Landscape Architecture* 84(10): 72–73.

Lovejoy, Sharon. 1991. *Sunflower Houses*. Loveland, CO: Interweave Press.

Lucas, Bill. 1995. "Learning through landscapes." *Children's Environments*. 12(2): 233–244.

Lyle, John T. 1994. *Regenerative Design for Sustainable Development*. New York: John Wiley & Sons.

Moore, Robin. 1990. *Childhood's Domain: Play and Place in Child Development*. Berkeley, CA: MIG Communications.

Nabhan, Gary P., and Stephen Trimble. 1994. *The Geography of Childhood: Why Children Need Natural Places*. Boston, MA: Beacon Press.

Severson, Rebecca. 1993. "United we sprout: a Chicago community garden story." In *The Meaning of Gardens*, edited by M. Francis and R. Hester. Cambridge, MA: MIT Press.

Titman, Wendy. 1994. *Special Places: Special People*. Surrey, United Kingdom: World Wide Fund for Nature/Learning Through Landscapes.

Zavitkovsky, Docia. 1996. "Docia shares a story about choices." *Child Care Information Exchange* (January): 79.

BIBLIOGRAPHY

Adams, Eileen. 1993. "School's out!: New initiatives for British school grounds." *Children's Environments* 19(2): 19–29.

Alexander, Christopher. 1979. *A Timeless Way of Building*. New York: Oxford University Press.

Alexander, Christopher, S. Ishikawa, and M. Silverstein. 1977 *A Pattern Language*. New York: Oxford University Press.

Alexander, Jacquelyn, Mary-Wales North, and Deborah K. Hendren. 1995. "Master gardener classroom garden project: An evaluation of the benefits to children." *Children's Environments* 12(2): 256–263.

Allen, Lady, of Hurtwood. 1968. *Planning for Play*. Cambridge, MA: MIT Press.

Altman, Irwin, and S. Low, eds. 1992. *Place Attachment*. New York: Plenum Press.

Altman, Irwin and J. Wohlwill, eds. 1978. *Children and the Environment*. New York: Plenum Press.

————. 1983. *Behavior and the Natural Environment*. New York: Plenum Press.

Anthony, Kathryn H. 1987. "Environment-behavior research applied to design: The case of Rosemead High School." *The Journal of Architectural and Planning Research* 4(2): 91–107.

Bachelad, G. 1964. *The Poetics of Space*. Boston, MA: Beacon Press.

Baker, Katherine R. 1974. *Let's Play Outdoors.* Washington DC: National Association for the Education of Young Children.

Baker, Robert L., and Birgitte R. Mednick. 1990. "Protecting the high school environment as an island of safety." *Children's Environments Quarterly,* 7(3): 37–49.

Baldassari, Carol, Sheila Lehman, and Maxine Wolfe. 1987. "Imagining and creating alternative environments with children." In *Spaces for Children: The Built Environment and Child Development,* edited by C. Weinstein and T. David. New York: Plenum Press.

Barker, Roger. 1968. *Ecological Psychology.* Palo Alto, CA: Stanford University Press.

Barker, Roger, and Paul Gump. 1964. *Big School, Small School.* Palo Alto, CA: Stanford University Press.

Bartlett, Sheridan. 1990. "Introduction." *Children's Environments Quarterly* 7(4): 3.

———. 1991. "Kids aren't like they used to be: Nostalgia and reality in neighborhood life." *Children's Environments Quarterly* 8(1): 49–58.

———. 1993. "Amiable space in the schools of Reggio Emilia: An interview with Lella Gandini." *Children's Environments* 10(2): 113–126.

Bengtsson, A. 1972. *Adventure Playgrounds.* New York: Praeger.

Blakely, Kim Susan. 1994. "Parents' conceptions of social dangers to children in the urban environment." *Children's Environments* 11(1): 16–25.

Bradley, Lucy. 1995. "Tierra Buena: The creation of an urban wildlife habitat in an elementary school in the inner city." *Children's Environments* 12(2): 245–249.

Brown, J., and C. Burger. 1984. "Playground designs and preschool children's behavior." *Environment and Behavior* 16: 599–626.

Bultimer, A., and D. Seamon, eds. 1980 *The Human Experience of Space and Place.* New York: St. Martins Press.

Burns, Jim. 1979. *Connections: Ways to Discover and Realize Community Potential.* San Francisco, CA: McGraw-Hill.

Burns, Jim, and Lawrence Halprin. 1974. *Taking Part: A Workshop: Approach to Collective Creativity.* Cambridge, MA: MIT Press,.

Buss, Shirl. 1995. "Urban Los Angeles from young people's angle of vision." *Children's Environments* 12(3): 340–351.

Carr, Stephen, Mark Francis, Leanne Rivlin, and Andrew Stone. 1992. *Public Space.* New York: Cambridge University Press.

Chawla, Louise. 1990. "Ecstatic places." *Children's Environments Quarterly* 7(4): 18–23.

———. 1992. "Childhood place attachments." In *Place Attachment,* edited by I. Altman and S. Low. New York: Plenum Press.

———. 1994. *In the First Country of Places: Nature, Poetry, and Childhood Memory.* Albany, NY: State University of New York Press.

Christoffel, Katherine K. 1995. "Handguns and the environments of children." *Children's Environments* 12(1): 39–48.

Cobb, Elizabeth. 1959. *The Ecology of Imagination in Childhood*. New York: Columbia University Press.

Cohen, Stewart, and Susan Trostle. 1990. "Young children's preferences for school-related physical-environmental setting characteristics." *Environment and Behavior* 22(6): 753–766.

Cohen, U., T. McGinty, and G. T. Moore. 1978. "Environment for Play and Childcare Project." Draft report to Pacific Oaks College and Children's School, Pacific Oaks Archives.

Cohen, Uriel, Ann Hill, Carol Lane, Tim McGinty, and Gary T. Moore. 1979. "Recommendations for child play areas." WI: Center for Architecture and Urban Planning Research, University of Wisconsin Press, Milwaukee.

Cooper Marcus, Clare. 1992. "Environmental memories." In *Place Attachment*, edited by I. Altman and S. Low. New York: Plenum Press.

Cooper Marcus, Clare, and Carolyn Francis, eds. 1990. *People Places: Design Guidelines for Urban Open Space*. New York: Van Nostrand Reinhold.

———. 1995. "Growing up in a danger zone: How modernization efforts can improve the environment of childhood in public housing." *Children's Environments*, 12(1): 57–64.

Corbishley, Peter. 1995. "A parish listens to its children." *Children's Environments*, 12(4): 414–426.

Cuff, D., and E. Robertson. 1983. "Words and images." *Journal of Architectural Education* 36: 8–15.

Cumming, J., and E. Cumming. 1962. *Ego and Milieu*. New York: Atherton Press.

Dattner, R. 1969. *Design for Play*. Cambridge, MA: MIT Press.

David, T., and B. Wright, eds. 1974. *Learning Environments*. Chicago, IL: University of Chicago Press.

Deasy, C. M. 1974. *Design for Human Affairs*. New York: John Wiley & Sons.

deConinck-Smith, Ning. 1990. "Where should children play? City planning seen from knee-height: Copenhagen 1870–1920. *Children's Environments Quarterly* 7(4): 54–61.

Dovey, Kimberly. 1990. "Refuge and imagination: Places of peace in childhood." *Children's Environments Quarterly* 7(4): 13–17.

Downing, Frances. 1989. *Image Banks*. Annarbor, MI: University of Michigan Press.

———. 1992. "The role of place and event imagery in the act of design." *The Journal of Architectural and Planning Research*, 9:1, 64–77.

Downs, R., and D. Stea, eds. 1973. *Image and Environment: Cognitive Mapping and Spatial Behavior*. Chicago, IL: Aldine.

Edwards, Carolyn, Lella Gandini, and George Forman, eds. 1993. *The Hundred Languages of Children*. Norwood, NJ: Ablex Publishing Corporation.

Ellison, Gail. 1974. *Play Structures—Questions to Discuss, Designs to Consider, Directions for Construction*. Pasadena, CA: Pacific Oaks College.

Eriksen, A. 1985. *Playground Design*. New York: Van Nostrand Reinhold.

Esbensen, Steen. 1987. *An Outdoor Classroom.* Ypsilanti, MI: High Scope Press.

Ferguson, Jerry. 1979. "Creating growth-producing environments for infants and toddlers." In *Supporting the Growth of Infants, Toddlers and Parents,* edited by Elizabeth Jones. Pasadena CA: Pacific Oaks College.

Flemming, R., and R. Von Tscharner. 1981. *Place Makers.* New York: Hastings House.

Francis, Carolyn. 1990. "Day care outdoor spaces." In *People Places: Design Guidelines for Urban Open Space,* edited by C. Cooper Marcus and C. Francis. New York: Van Nostrand Reinhold.

Francis, Mark. 1995. "Childhood's garden: Memory and meaning of gardens." *Children's Environments,* 12(2): 183–191.

Francis, Mark, and Randolph Hester, eds. 1993. *The Meaning of Gardens.* Cambridge, MA: MIT Press.

Freeman, Claire. 1995. Planning and play: Creating greener environments." *Children's Environments.* 12(3): 383–388.

Frost, Joe L., and Barry Klein. 1979. *Children's Play and Playgrounds.* Boston, MA: Allyn and Bacon.

Frost, Joe L., and Sylvia Sunderlin, eds. 1985. *When Children Play.* Wheaton, MD: Association for Childhood Education International.

Galvin, Michael. 1993. "The Columbine School: A principlal reflects on the influence of school design." *Children's Environments* 10(2): 154–158.

Gandini, Lella. 1991. "Not just anywhere: Making child care centers into 'particular' places." *Exchange* (March/April): 5–9.

——. 1993. "Educational and caring spaces." In *The Hundred Languages of Children,* edited by C. Edwards, L. Gandini, and G. Forman. Norwood, NJ: Ablex.

Gauldie, Sinclair. 1969. *Architecture: The Appreciation of the Arts.* London: Oxford University Press.

Greenbie, B. B. 1981. *Spaces: Dimensions of the Human Landscape.* New Haven, CT: Yale University Press.

Greenman, Jim. 1988. *Caring Spaces, Learning Places: Children's Environments That Work.* Redmond, WA: Exchange Press.

Gross, R., and J. Murphy. 1968. *Educational Change and Architectural Consequences.* Milwaukee, WI: Educational Facilities Laboratory.

Groves, Mark, and Claire Mason. 1993. "The relationship between preference and environment in the school playground." *Children's Environments* 10(1): 52–59.

Guilfoil, Joanne. 1992. "Art and built environment education: Sidewalks as art education." *Art Education* (September): 24.

Hall, E. T. 1969. *The Hidden Dimension.* New York: Doubleday.

Harms, Thelma. 1994. "Humanizing infant environments for group care." *Children's Environments* 11(2): 155–167.

Hart, Roger. 1974. "The genesis of landscaping." *Landscape Architecture* 65(5): 356–363.

———. 1979. *Children's Experience of Place.* New York: Irvington Press.

———. 1992. *Children's Participation: From Tokenism to Citizenship. Innocenti Essays* No. 4. Florence, Italy: UNICEF International Child Development Center.

Harvey, Margarete R. 1989. "Children's experiences with vegetation. *Children's Environments Quarterly,* 6(1): 36–43.

Heffernan, Maureen. 1994. "The children's garden project at river farm." *Children's Environments* 11(3): 221–231.

Heseltine, Peter, and John Holborn. 1987. *Playgrounds.* New York: Nichols Publishing.

Hester, R. T. 1985. "Subconscious landscapes in the heart." *Places* 2:3: 10–22.

———. 1990. *Community Design Primer.* Mendocino, CA: Ridge Times Press.

Hill, Dorothy. 1977. *Mud, Sand and Water.* Washington, DC: National Association for the Education of Young Children.

Hillman, M., J. Adams, and J. Witlegg. 1990. *One False Move . . . A Study of Children's Independent Mobility.* London: The Policy Studies Institute.

Hiss, T. 1987. "Reflections: Experiencing places." *The New Yorker* 22 June, 46–68; 29 June, 73–86.

Huttenmoser, Marco. 1995. "Children and their living surroundings: Empirical investigations into the significance of living surroundings for the everyday life and development of children." *Children's Environments* 12(4): 403–413.

Jones, Elizabeth. 1977. *Dimensions of Teaching-Learning Environments.* Pasadena, CA: Pacific Oaks College.

Jones, Elizabeth, eds. 1978. *Joys and Risks in Teaching Young Children.* Pasadena, CA: Pacific Oaks College.

———. 1979. *Supporting the Growth of Infants, Toddlers and Parents.* Pasadena, CA: Pacific Oaks College.

Jones, Elizabeth, and Elizabeth Prescott. 1978. *Dimensions of Teaching Learning Environments. II. Focus on Day Care.* Pasadena, CA: Pacific Oaks College.

Jones, Elizabeth, and Gretchen Reynolds. 1992. *The Play's the Thing.* New York: Teachers College Press.

Kaplan, Rachel, and Stephen Kaplan. 1989. *The Experience of Nature.* Cambridge, MA: Cambridge University Press.

———. 1993. "Restorative experience: The healing power of nearby nature." In *The Meaning of Gardens,* edited by M. Francis and R. Hester. Cambridge, MA: The MIT Press.

King, Stanley. 1989. *Co-Design.* New York: Van Nostrand Reinhold.

Kinn, Chris. 1989. "Ingredients for a living school." *Children's Environments Quarterly* 6(1): 44–45.

Kirkby, MaryAnn. 1989. "Nature as refuge in children's environments." *Children's Environments Quarterly,* 6(1): 7–12.

Kritchevsky, Sybil, and Elizabeth Prescott. 1969. *Planning Environments for Young Children: Physical Space.* Washington, DC: National Association for the Education of Young Children.

Lang, Jon. 1987. *Creating Architectural Theory: The Role of the Behavioral Scientist in Environmental Design.* New York: Van Nostrand Reinhold.

Learning Through Landscapes. 1995. "E-scape." *Learning Through Landscapes Newsletter* 8 (June).

Leccese, Michael. 1995. "Redefining the idea of play." *Landscape Architecture* 84(10): 72–73.

Lindbery, L. 1986. *Facility Design for Early Childhood Programs.* Washington, DC: National Association for the Education of Young Children.

Loughlin, Catherine, and Joseph Suina. 1982. *The Learning Environment: An Instructional Strategy.* New York: Teachers College Press.

Lovejoy, Sharon. 1991. *Sunflower Houses: Garden Discoveries for Children of All Ages.* Loveland, CO: Interweave Press.

Lucas, Bill. 1995. "Learning through landscapes." *Children's Environments* 12(2): 233–244.

Lyle, John T. 1994. *Regenerative Design for Sustainable Development.* New York: John Wiley and Sons.

Lynch, Kevin. 1960. *The Image of the City.* Cambridge, MA: MIT Press.

———. 1981. *A Theory of Good City Form.* Cambridge, MA: MIT Press.

Lynch, Kevin, and A. Lukashok. 1956. "Some childhood memories of the city." *Journal of the American Institute of Planners* 22(3): 142–152.

Mason, Rachel. 1994. "Artistic achievement in Japanese junior high schools." *Art Education* (January): 8–18.

Massad, C. 1979. "Time and space in space and time." In *Children in Time and Space,* edited by K. Tamamoto. New York: Teachers College Press.

Milne, A. A. 1973. *When We Were Very Young.* New York: Penguin.

Mitchell, Edna, and R. Anderson. 1980. "Play spaces in Denmark." *Young Children* 35(2): 2–8.

Moore, Gary T. 1985. "State of the art in play environment." in *When Children Play,* edited by J. Frost and S. Sunerlin. Wheaton, MD: Association of Childhood Education International, 171–192.

Moore, Gary T., and Jeffrey Lackney. 1993. "School design: Crisis, educational performance and design applications. " *Children's Environments* 10(2): 99–112.

Moore, Robin. 1989. "Before and after asphalt: Diversity as an ecological measure of quality in children's outdoor environments." In *The Ecological Context of Children's Play,* edited by M. Bloch and A. Pellirini. Norwood, NJ: Ablex.

———.1990. *Childhood's Domain: Play and Place in Child Development.* Berkeley CA: MIG Communications.

———. 1993. *Plants for Play.* Berkeley, CA: MIG Communications.

————. 1995. "Children gardening: First steps towards a sustainable future. *Children's Environments* 12(2): 222–231.

Moore, Robin, and Donald Young. 1978. "Childhood outdoors: Toward a social ecology of the landscape." In *Children and the Environment*, edited by I. Altman and J. Wohlwill. New York: Plenum Press.

Moore, Robin, S. Goltsman, and D. Iacofano, eds. 1987. *Play for All Guidelines.* Berkeley, CA: MIG Communications.

Nabhan, Gary P., and Stephen Trimble. 1994. *The Geography of Childhood: Why Children Need Natural Places.* Boston, MA: Beacon Press.

Nelson, Doreen, and Jule Sundt. 1993. "Changing the architecture of teacher's minds." *Children's Environments* 10(2): 159–169.

Nicholson, Simon. 1971. "How not to cheat children, the theory of loose parts." *Landscape Architecture* 62(1): 30–34.

Olds, Anita Rui. 1989. "Nature as healer." *Children's Environments Quarterly* 6(1): 27–32.

Olwig, Kenneth R. 1990. "Designs upon children's special places." *Children's Environments Quarterly* 7(4): 47–53.

————. 1991. "Childhood, artistic creation, and the educated sense of place." *Children's Environments Quarterly* 8(2): 4–18.

————. 1993. "Harmony, 'quintessence', and, children's acquisition of concern for the 'natural environment.' *Children's Environments* 10(1): 60–71.

Osmon, Fred L. 1973. *Patterns for Designing Children's Centers.* New York: Educational Facilities Laboratories.

Owens, P. 1988. "Natural landscapes, gathering places and prospect refuges: Characteristics of outdoor places valued by teens." *Children's Environments Quarterly* 5: 17–24.

Paull, Dorothy, and John Paull. 1972. *Yesterday I Found . . . .* Boulder, CO: University of Colorado Press.

Pedersen, Jens. 1985. "The adventure playgrounds of Denmark." In *When Children Play*, edited by J. Frost and S. Sunderlin. MD: Association of Childhood Education International, 201–208.

Pennartz, Paul, and M. Elsinga. 1990. "Adults', adolescents', and architects' differences in perception of the urban environment." *Environment and Behavior* 22(15): 675–714.

Prescott, Elizabeth. 1975. *Assessment of Child-Rearing Environments: An Ecological Approach.* Pasadena, CA: Pacific Oaks College.

————. 1984. "The physical setting in day care." In *Making Day Care Better*, edited by J. Greenman and R. Fuqua. New York: Teachers College Press.

Prescott, Elizabeth. 1987. "The environment as an organizer of intent in child-care settings." In *Spaces for Children: The Built Environment and Child Development*, edited by C. Weinstein and T. David. New York: Plenum Press.

Prescott, Elizabeth, and Elizabeth Jones. 1972. *Day Care as a Child-Rearing Environment.* Vol. II. Washington, DC: National Association for the Education of Young Children.

Proshansky, Harold, and Abbe Fabian. 1987. "The development of place identity in the child." In *Spaces for Children*, edited by C. Weinstein and T. David. New York: Plenum Press.

Proshansky, Harold, Abbe Fabian, and R. Kamenoff. 1983. "Place and identity." *Journal of Environmental Psychology*. (3): 57–83.

Raymund, Judi Ferrel. 1995. "From barnyards to backyards: An exploration through adult memories and children's narratives in search of an ideal playscape." *Children's Environments* 12(3): 362–380.

Relph, E. 1976. *Place and Placelessness.* London: Pion.

Rivkin, Mary S. 1995. *The Great Outdoors.* Washington, DC: National Association for the Education of Young Children.

Rivlin, L., and M. Wolfe. 1985. *Institutional Settings in Children's Lives.* New York: John Wiley & Sons.

Rossi, Aldo. 1981. *A Scientific Autobiography.* Cambridge, MA: MIT Press.

Rudofsky, B. 1964. *Architecture Without Architects.* New York: Doubleday.

Sanoff, Henry. 1993. "Designing a responsive school environment." *Children's Environments* 10(2): 140–153.

Sarason, Seymour. 1971. *The Culture of the School and the Problems of Change.* Boston, MA: Allyn and Bacon.

Sebba, Rachel. 1991. "The landscapes of childhood." *Environment and Behavior* 32(4): 395–421.

Simmons, Deborah A. 1994. "Urban children's preferences for nature: Lessons for environmental education." *Children's Environments* 11(3): 194–203.

Smith, Fiona. 1995. "Children's voices and the construction of children's spaces: The example of playcare centers in the United Kingdom." *Children's Environments* 12(3): 389–396.

Sobel, David. 1990. "A place in the world: Adults' memories of childhood's special places." *Children's Environment Quarterly* 7(4): 5–12.

————. 1993. *Children's Special Places: Exploring the Role of Forts, Dens and Bush Houses in Middle Childhood.* Tucson, AZ: Zephyr Press.

Sommer, Barbara. 1990. "Favorite places of Estonian adolescents." *Children's Environments Quarterly* 7(4): 32–36.

Stevenson, H., H. Azuma, and K. Hakuta, eds. 1986. *Child Development and Education in Japan.* New York: W. H. Freeman.

Stine, Sharon. 1973. *Supporting Change in Public Schools.* Pasadena, CA: Pacific Oaks College.

Stine, Sharon, ed. 1983. *Administration: A Bedside Guide.* Pasadena, CA: Pacific Oaks College.

Stine, Sharon. 1993. "Shaping and being shaped by the environment." *Junge Kinder* 22(1): 17–21.

Stine, Sharon, and Elizabeth Jones. 1983. "Feedback: A two-way process." In *On the Growing Edge*, edited by Elizabeth Jones. Pasadena, CA: Pacific Oaks College.

Stine, Sharon., Kathleen Bullard, and Lew Kemble. 1993. "Engaging high school students in the development of a master plan for their campus: Listening, Playing and 'hanging-out.'" *EDRA 24*, (March): 152–157.

Sutton-Smith, Brian. 1985. *Learning Through the Built Environment: An Ecological Approach to Child Development.* New York: Irvington.

————. 1990. "School playground as festival." *Children's Environments Quarterly* 7(2): 3–7.

Taylor, Anne. 1993. "The learning environment as a three-dimensional textbook." *Children's Environments* 10(2): 170–179.

Titman, Wendy. 1994. *Special Places; Special People.* Surrey, United Kingdom: World Wide Fund for Nature/Learning through Landscapes.

Tobin, Joseph J., David Y. H. Wu, and Dana H. Davidson. 1989. *Preschool in Three Cultures: Japan, China and the U.S.A.* New Haven Connecticut: Yale University Press.

Tuan, Yi-fu. 1980. "Rootedness vs. sense of place." *Landscape* 24: 3–8.

van Andel, Joost. 1990 "Places children like, dislike, and fear." *Children's Environments Quarterly* 7(4): 24–31.

Wals, Arjen E. 1994. "Nobody planted it, it just grew! Young adolescents' perceptions and experiences of nature in the context of urban environmental education. *Children's Environments* 11(3): 177–193.

Walsh, Prue. 1988. *Early Childhood Playgrounds.* Watson, Australia: Australian Early Childhood Association.

Walter, Eugene V. 1988. *Placeways.* Raleigh, NC: University of North Carolina.

Weinstein, Carol, and Thomas David. 1987. *Spaces for Children: The Built Environment and Child Development.* New York: Plenum Press.

Whyte, William. 1980. *The Social Life of Small Urban Spaces.* Washington, DC: The Conservation Foundation.

Whiren, Alice. 1995. "Planning a garden from a child's perspective." *Children's Environments* 12(2): 250–255.

Wilkinson, P. F. 1980. *Innovations in Play Environments.* New York: St. Martin's Press.

Wohlwill, J. F., and H. Heft. 1987. "The physical environment and the development of the child." In *Handbook of Environmental Psychology.* Vol. 1., edited by D. Stkols and I. Altman. New York: John Wiley.

Wood, Denis. 1993. "Ground to stand on: Some notes on kids' dirt play." *Children's Environments* 10(1): 3–18.

Zeisel, John. 1981. *Inquiry by Design.* New York: Cambridge University Press.

Zube, E., and G. Moore, eds., 1991. *Advances in Environment, Behavior and Design.* Vol. 3. New York: Plenum Press.

INDEX